POETIC LANDSCAPES

Watercolour Paintings by Patricia A. Evans

Foreword by Gladys Mary Coles

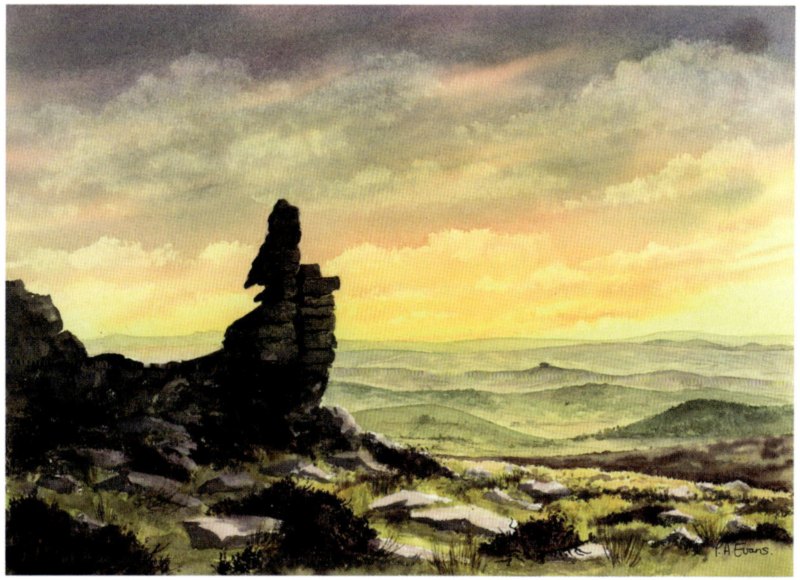

With quotations from the work of Mary Webb

TANKERVILLE GALLERY

Published by
TANKERVILLE GALLERY
Pennerley
Nr. Minsterley
Shropshire SY5 ONB

ISBN 0-9542994- 0-X

Printed in England by Precision Colour Printing Ltd, Haldane, Halesfield 1, Telford. TF7 4QQ

Front cover - View from Manstone Stiperstones towards Bromlow Callow & Wales

Dedicated to the memory of my parents, Bill and Edna Breeze

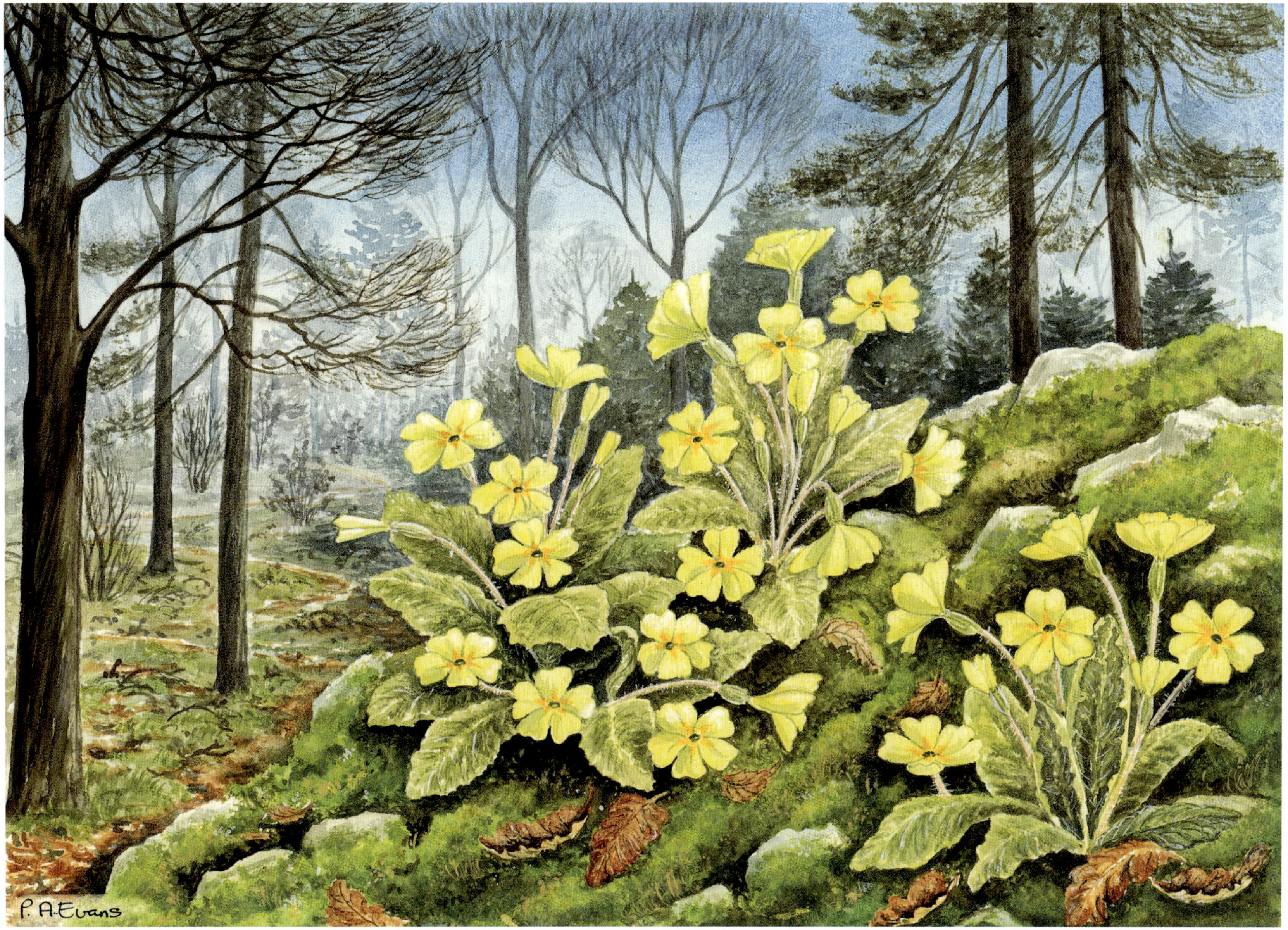

POEMS and PROSE

Poems reprinted from *Selected Poems of Mary Webb* (Headland)

Edited by Gladys Mary Coles

PAINTINGS

ACKNOWLEDGEMENTS

My appreciation and thanks for writing the Foreword to this book go to Gladys Mary Coles, who is the biographer of Mary Webb and President of the Mary Webb Society. I am indebted to her for permission to use the poetry from her book *Selected Poems of Mary Webb* (Headland), also for assistance in selecting the prose, and for her constant enthusiasm for the book.

I would also like to give my appreciation and thanks to Noel for layout and setting up the text, to Philip for proof-reading, to Simon for being a useful critic, and to Roy for introducing me to the South Shropshire Hills.

Finally my appreciation goes to my parents for instilling within me a great love of the countryside.

FOREWORD

It gives me great pleasure to introduce the watercolour paintings of Patricia Evans, collected for the first time in this book. I know that her work will enchant lovers of the countryside, especially lovers of Shropshire and the Welsh Border landscape. For Patricia Evans, this countryside is her primary source of inspiration. A trained artist, who has exhibited widely, she has lived in the South Shropshire hills for most of her adult life and her intimacy with this natural environment is clearly reflected in her work, in its fine detail and evocation of atmosphere, seasons and moods.

It is not surprising that Patricia Evans draws inspiration from Shropshire`s supreme verbal artist Mary Webb, who in her novels, poetry and essays conjures richly and hauntingly the border countryside. In this delightful book of landscape art, the paintings are matched and complemented by extracts from Mary Webb`s poetry and prose.

Mary Webb (1881-1927) is best known for her six novels, notably *Precious Bane* (1924) and *Gone to Earth* (1917), all set in Shropshire. She also wrote poetry throughout her life, although her work was not gathered in a published collection until after her death. These are reflective and perceptive poems, redolent of the Shropshire countryside with which her spirit was entwined. A full, chronological edition of her poetry is available today in my book, *Selected Poems of Mary Webb* (Headland).

The magical combination of art and literature in these pages make *Poetic Landscapes* a double source of pleasure, a timeless and rich feast.

Gladys Mary Coles

THE HILLS OF HEAVEN

We were in the hills of heaven
But yesterday!
All was so changeless, quiet, fair,
All swam so deep in golden air;
White-tapered chestnuts, seven by seven,
Went down the shady valleys there
Where daffodils are, and linnets play;
And singing streams of yellow and brown
Through golden mimulus ran down.
Ah, haunted were the hills of heaven,
Where no tree falls and none is riven,
Where the frail valley-lilies stay
Becalmed in beauty, every leaf
And every flower! Ah, bitter grief -
Remembering the hills of heaven
And yesterday !

M. W.

Dawn - Stiperstones from Bromlow Callow

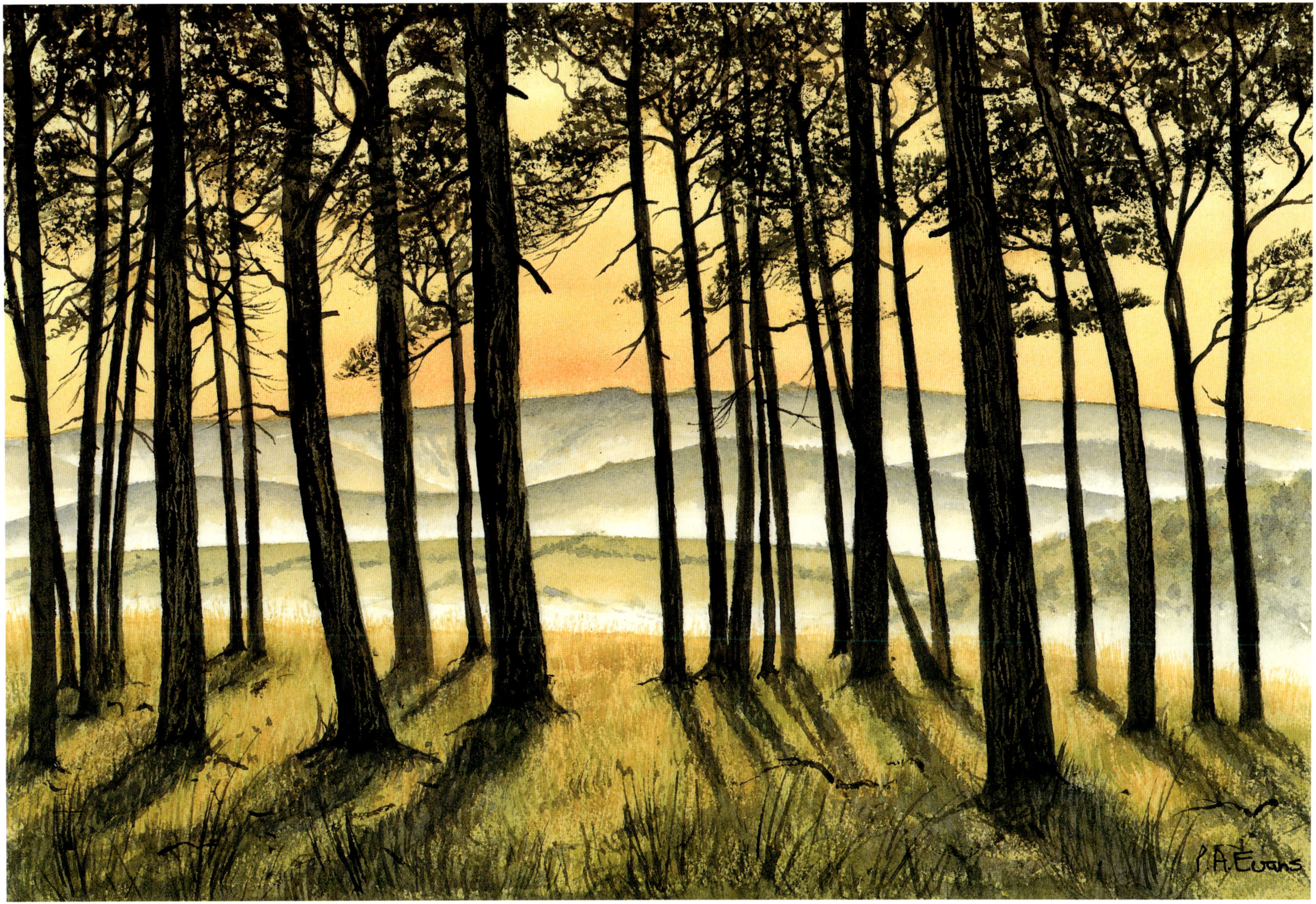
P.A. Evans

HILL PASTURES

High on the hill the curlews and the whimbrels,
Go mating all day long with a sweet whistle;
With a sound of chiming bells and shaken timbrels,
And silver rings that fall in a crystal cup.
They laugh, as lovers laugh when the moon is up,
Over the cotton-grass and the carline thistle.

Poised in his airy spiral the snipe is calling,
Summoning love with a music, mournful and lonely
As a lost lamb in the night, rising, falling,
Stranger than any melody, wilder than song.
He cries of life that is short, and death that is long,
Telling his dusky love to one heart only.

Once in seven days a plaintive ringing
Sounds from a little chapel high in the heather,
Out with the sorrowful snipe and the whimbrel winging
The wild hill ponies hear it there as they graze,
And whinny, and call to their foals, and stand at gaze,
Hearing a clear voice in the clear weather.

And out of pine-dark farms and windy places,
And quiet cottages low in the valley hiding,
Brown folk come with still and wistful faces.
Straying by twos and threes, like the peaceful sheep,
Into the small brown shippen of souls they creep,
Seeking a calm like the hills, but more abiding.

M. W.

Lords Hill Chapel, Stiperstones

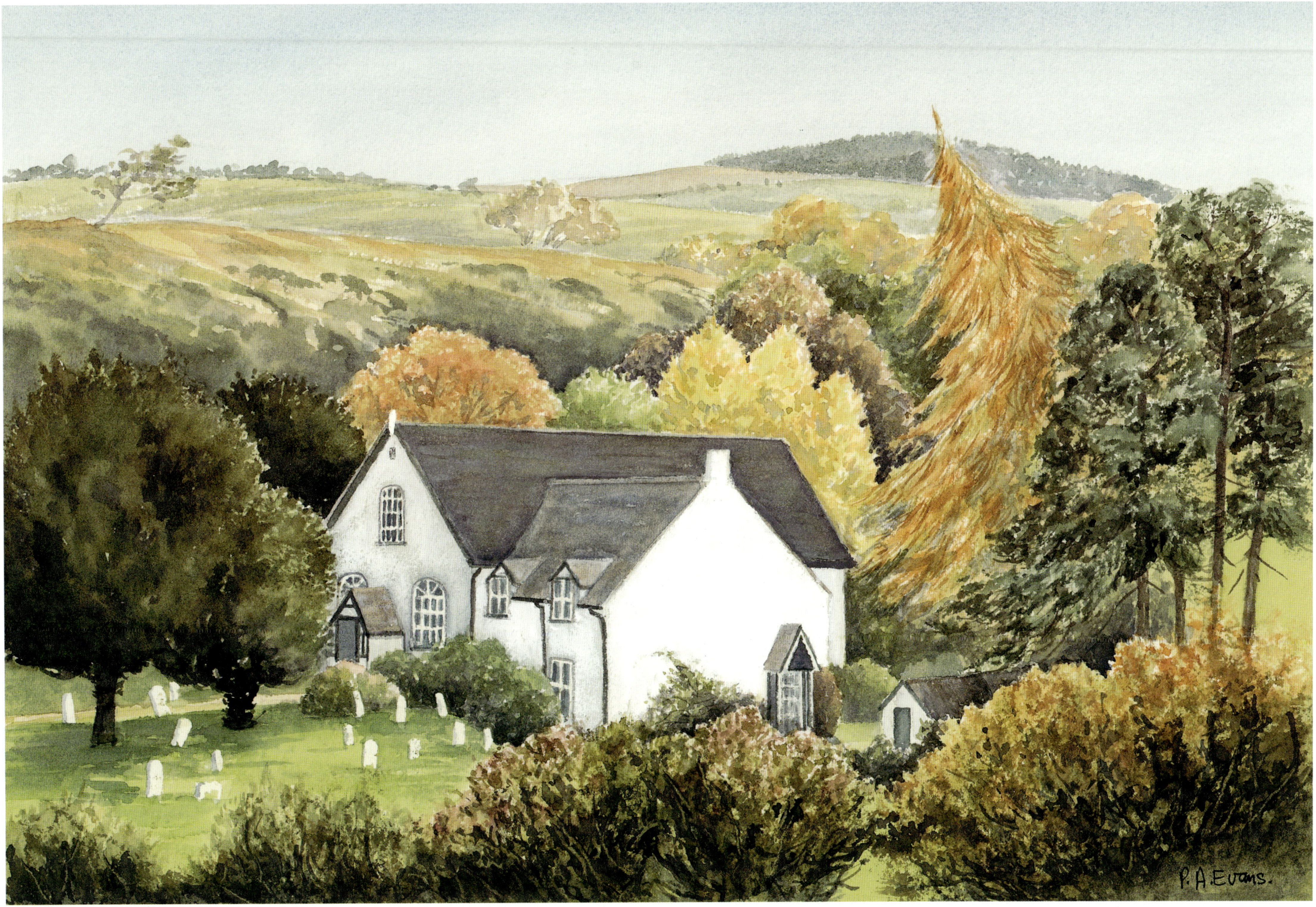
P. A. Evans.

THE LITTLE HILL

This is the hill, ringed by the misty shire -
The mossy, southern hill,
The little hill where larches climb so high.
Among the stars aslant
They chant;
Along the purple lower slopes they lie
In lazy golden smoke, more faint, more still
Than the pale woodsmoke of the cottage fire.
Here some calm Presence takes me by the hand
And all my heart is lifted by the chant
Of them that lean aslant
In golden smoke and sing, and softly bend:
And out from every larch-bole steals a friend.

M W

Pontesford Hill (before plantation)

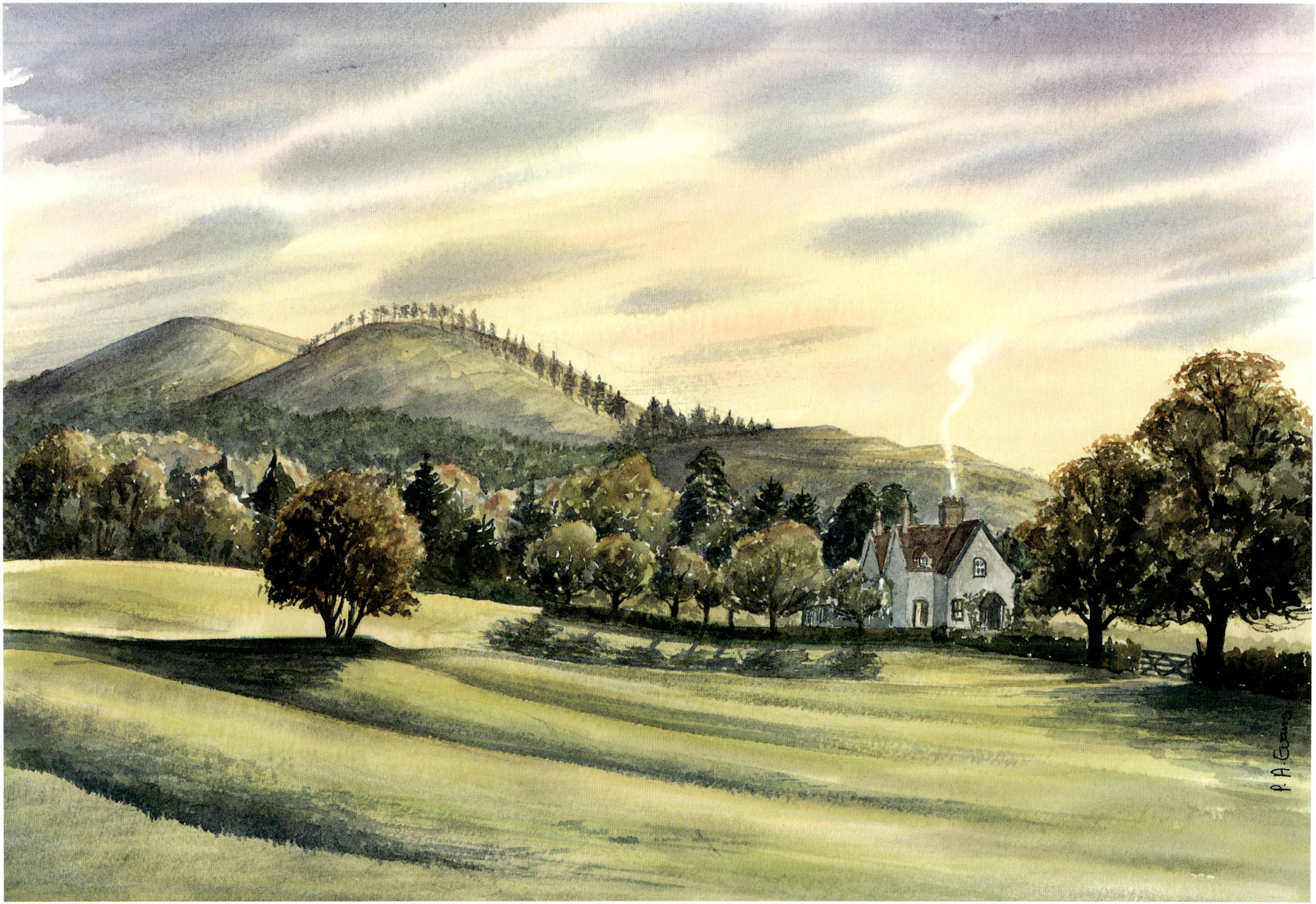
P. A. Evans

MOONLIGHT

A sharp young moon sidled up... entangled herself in the black manes of the pines which swayed a little in the rising night wind, slipped through them like a fish through a torn net, and swam free in a large grey sky which was beginning to tingle, between the woolly clouds, with a phosphorescence of faint starlight. In the last meadow that sloped up... Robert found the sheep, uneasy beneath a dubious heaven. They lay with their dim raddled bodies outlined by crisp, frosty, faintly luminous grass.

from *Seven for a Secret*

Pontesford Hill from the Nags Head (before plantation)

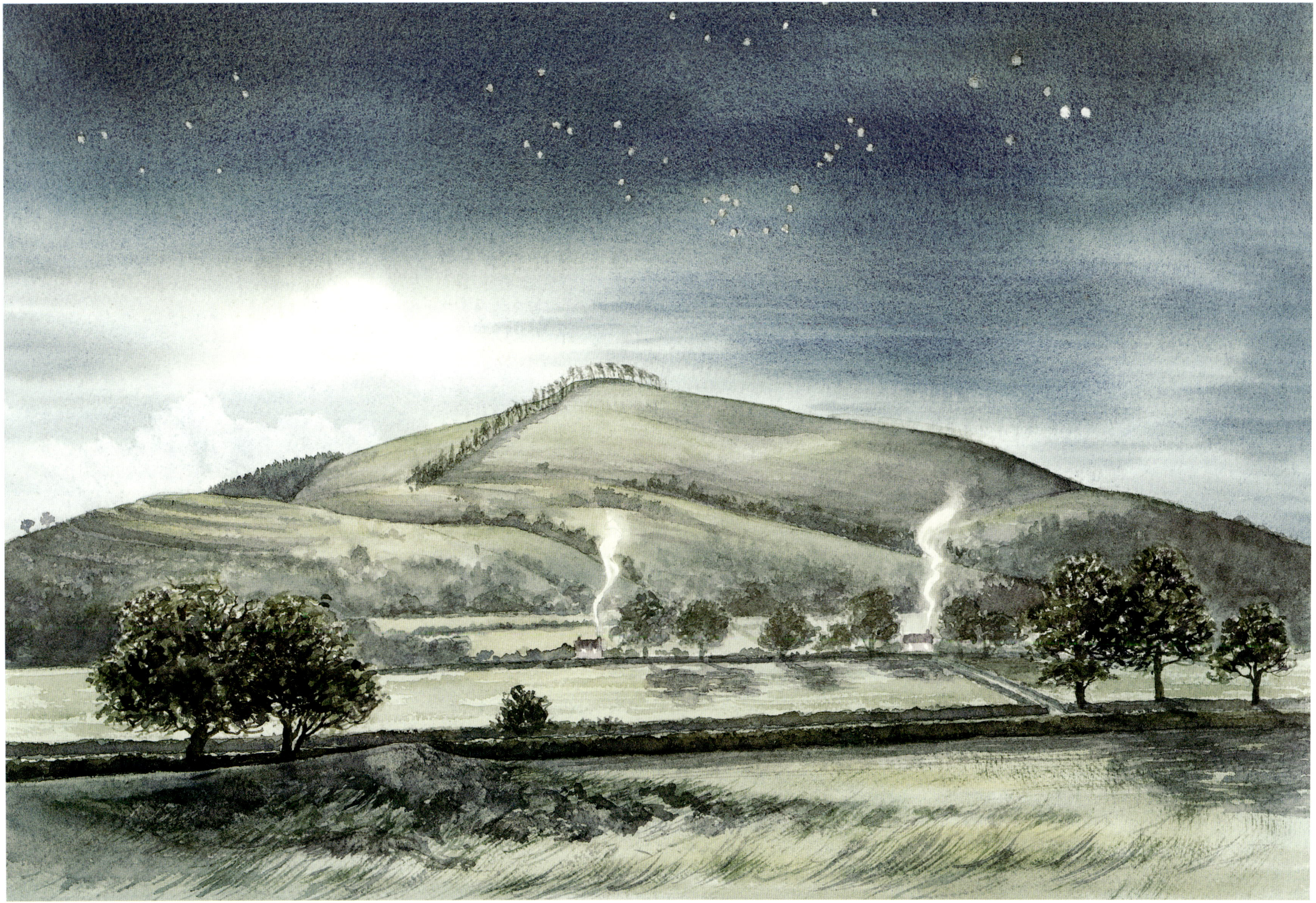

ON THE GREEN LONELY HILLS

On the green, lonely hills the sheep grazed with their lambs, and the air was never empty of their sweet, sad calling. In the warm plain the May hedges were already in flower... Once more the bracken pushed out soft fingers, and cuckoos cried from orchards at the foot of the cwms. The snipe summoned his love from his airy circles, and the curlews ran along the hilltops with their forlorn, elfin music.

from *The Golden Arrow*

View from Long Mynd toward the Wrekin

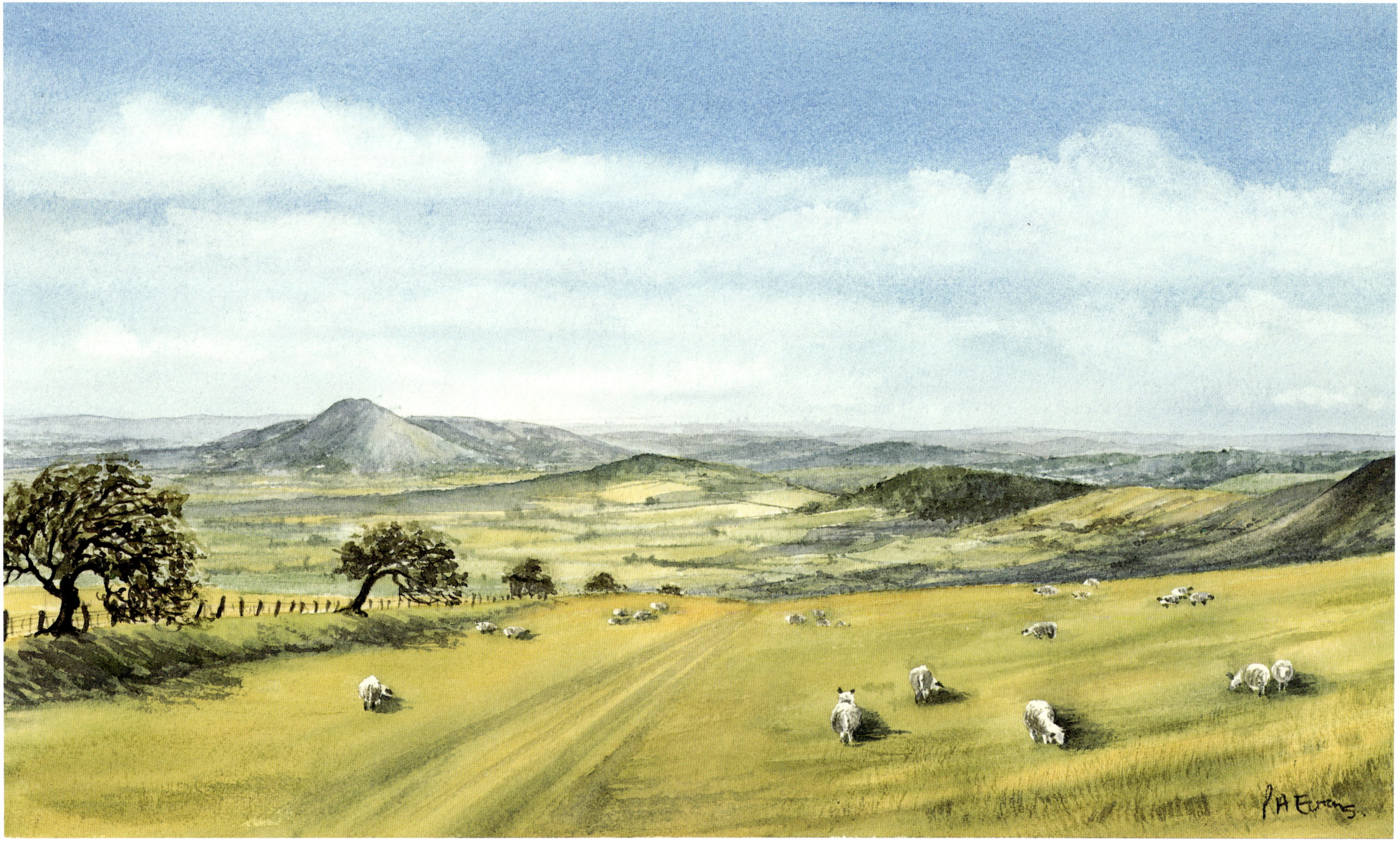
P H Evans.

MARKET DAY

Who'll walk the fields with us to town,
In an old coat and a faded gown?
We take our roots and country sweets
Where high walls shade the steep old streets,
And golden bells and silver chimes
Ring up and down the sleepy times.
The morning mountains smoke like fires;
The sun spreads out his shining wires;
The mower in the half-mown leasur
Sips his tea and takes his pleasure.
Along the lanes slow waggons amble;
The sad-eyed calves awake and gamble;
The foal that lay so sorrowful
Is playing in the grasses cool.
By slanting ways, in slanting sun,
Through startled lapwings now we run
Along the pale green hazel-path,
Through April's lingering aftermath
Of lady's smock and lady's slipper;
We stay to watch a nesting dipper.
The rabbits eye us while we pass,
Out of the sorrel-crimson grass;
The blackbird sings, without a fear,
Where honeysuckle horns blow clear -
Cool ivory stained with true vermilion;
And here, within a silk pavilion,
Small caterpillars lie at ease.
The endless shadows of the trees
Are painted purple and cobalt;
Grandiloquent, the rook-files halt,
Each one aware of you and me,
And full of conscious dignity.
Our shoes are golden as we pass
With pollen from the pansied grass.
Beneath an elder – set anew
With large clean plates to catch the dew –
On fine white cheese and bread we dine:
The clear brook-water tastes like wine.
If all folk lived with labour sweet
Of their own busy hands and feet,
Such marketing, it seems to me,
Would make an end of poverty.

M. W.

On the road to Shrewsbury

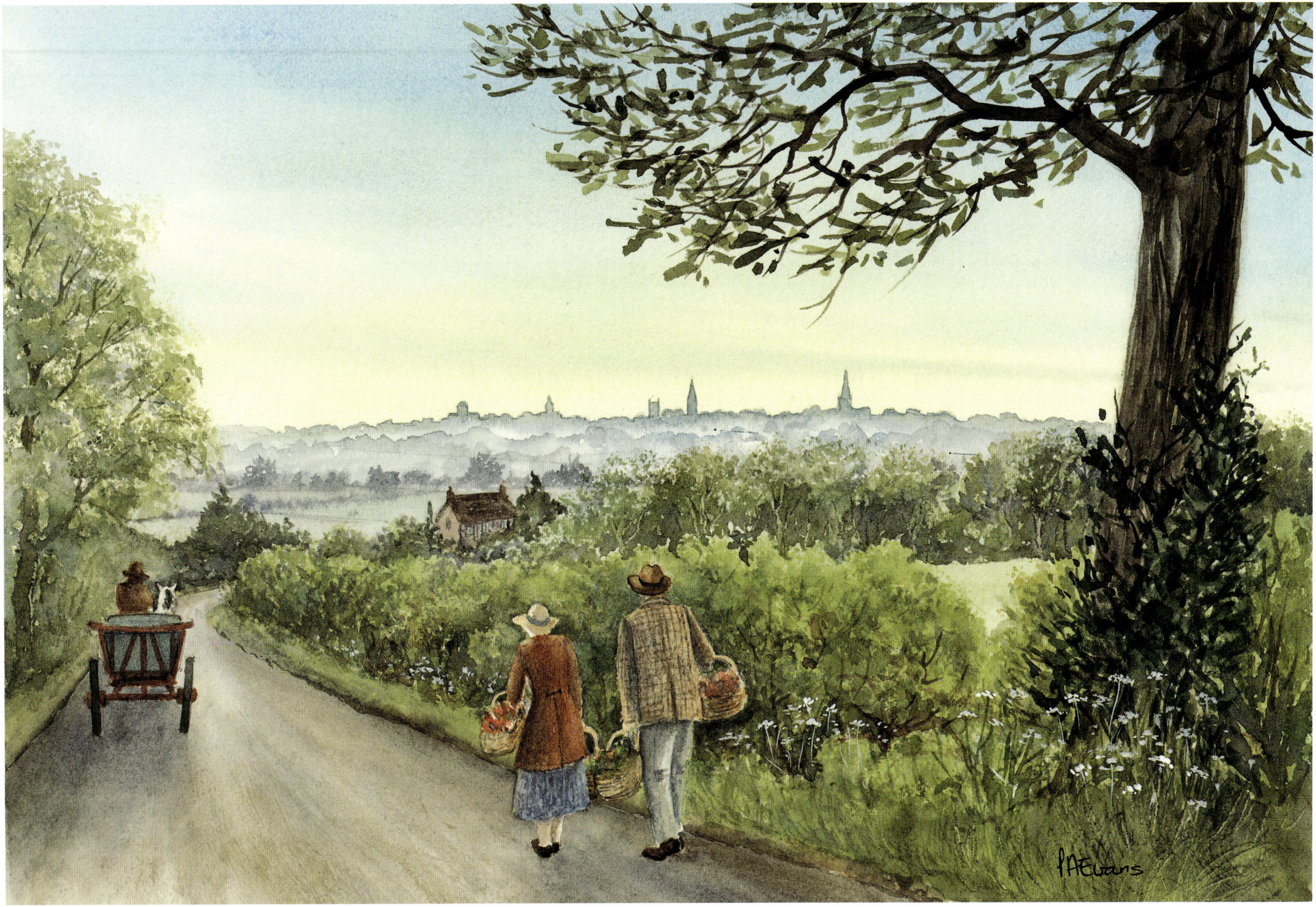
PAEvans

BROMLOW CALLOW

Small feckless clouds were hurried across the vast untroubled sky – shepherdless, futile, imponderable...
It was cold in the Callow – a spinney of silver birches and larches that topped a round hill.

from *Gone To Earth.*

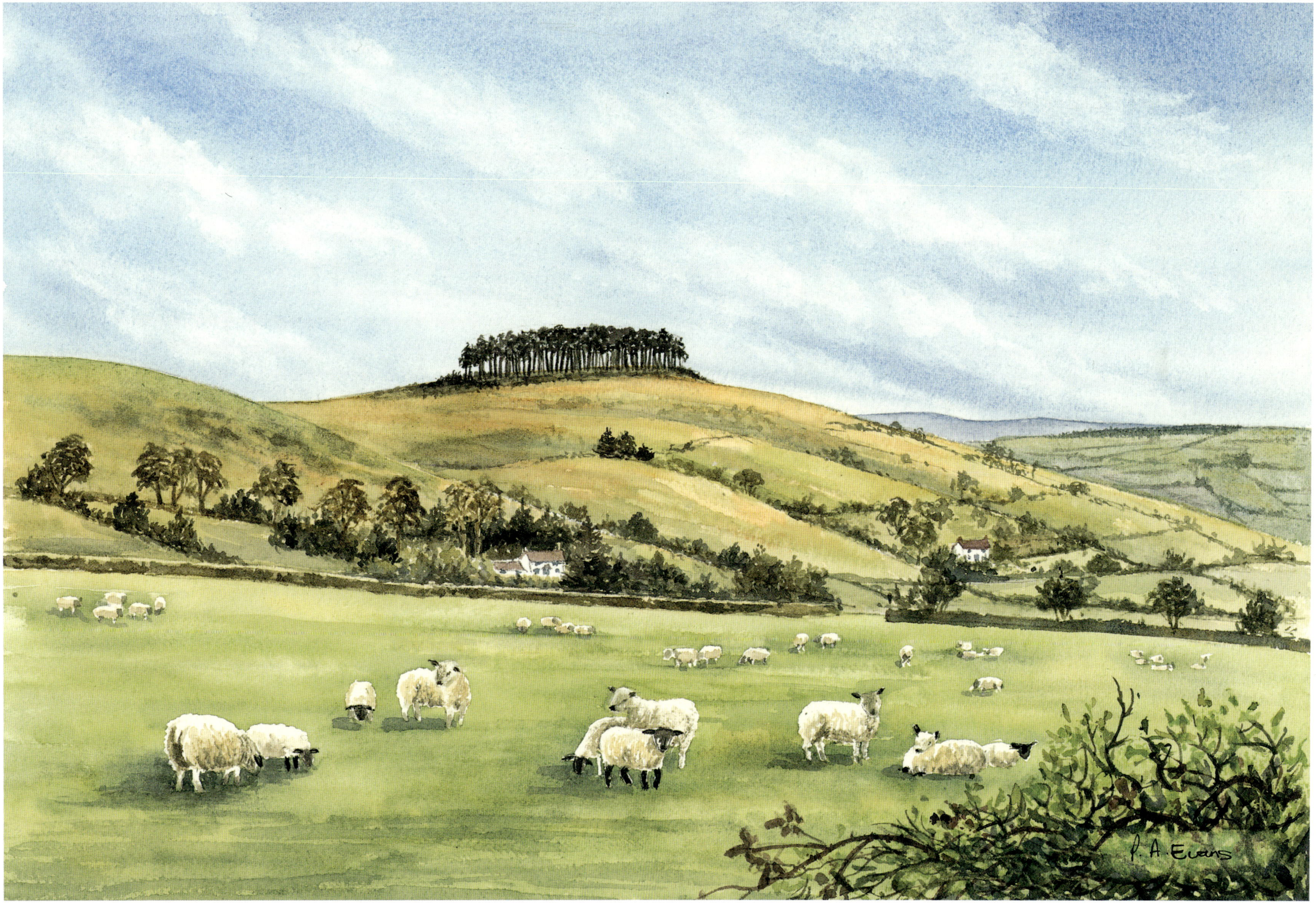
P. A. Evans

THE WOOD

Tall, feathered birches, on the tides of air,
Wash to and fro, like seaweeds fine and fair,
And deep in leaf and blossom from all eyes
The rope-walk of the honeysuckle lies.
There, crimson foxgloves taper slenderly,
And the brown-seeded brake grows ten feet high.
There are strange, flaming toadstools, and the berries
Of ash and rose, that shine like scarlet cherries.
The rose-bay willow herb, in her bridal hour,
Blooms, and the larch sets forth her rosy flower.
Kestrels are there, and tawny foxes play
Amid the shadows in the early day.
Low cry the sheep, and leave their shining fleece
On the long vines of purple blackberries.
High in their minstrel gallery above,
Hidden in fretted leaves, dove answers dove,
And like a distant bell, melodiously
Haunting these glades, the music of the bee
Chimes all summer. . . . Like a bird, with wings
Dusky and silent, I would flit through spring's
Wistful, immaculate colours; through the dream
And hush of summer; down the rush and gleam
Of autumn; and when winter, with a moan,
Swept through the freezing wood aloof, alone,
Prisoning the pine needles in shining, hollow
Cases of ice, yet the brown bird would follow.
Light as last year's leaf I'd flutter by,
With the sad note of finches in July.
Still should the foxgloves gather, spring by spring;
Still should the feathered birches wash and swing
Upon the tides of air, and in the sun
Each autumn should the little foxes run,
While I in shadow dwelt. Dark on the sky
Should kestrels anchor, watching warily
For small brown birds: but in the meadow green
I'd fearless flit, beneath their gaze unseen.

M. W.

Spring Coppice Lyth Hill

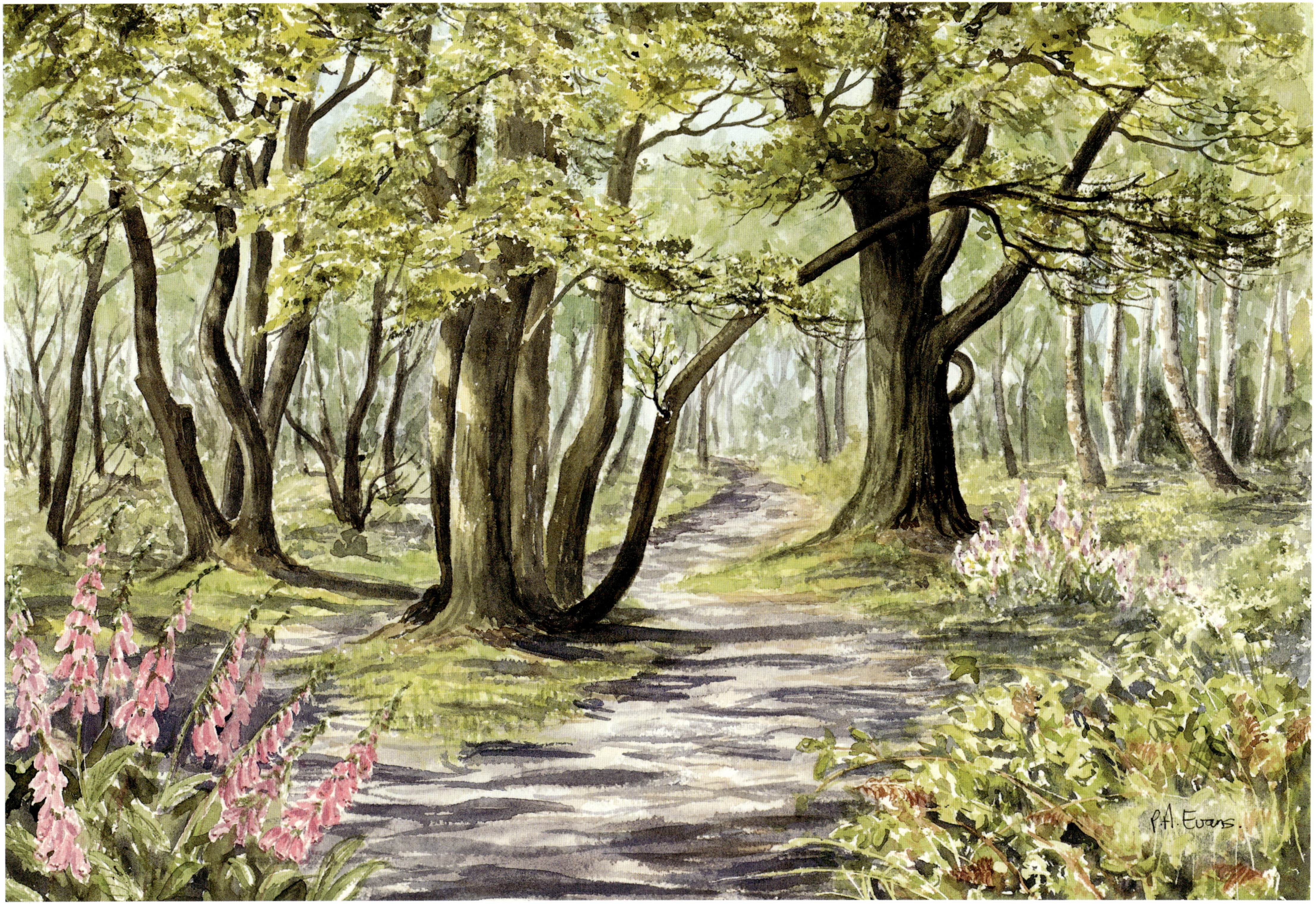
P.A. Evans.

PRESENCES

There is a presence on the lonely hill,
Lovely and chill:
There is an emanation in the wood,
Half understood.
They come upon me like an evening cloud,
Stranger than moon-rise, whiter than a shroud.
I shall not see them plain
Ever again,
Though in my childhood days
I knew their ways.
They are as secret as the black cloud-shadows
Sliding along the ripe midsummer grass;
With a breath-taking majesty they pass,
Down by the water in the mournful meadows;
Out of the pale pink distance at the falling
Of dusk they gaze - remote, summoning, chill;
Sweetly in April I have heard them calling
Where through black ash-buds gleams the purple hill.

M.W.

Huglith and Stiperstones from Lyth Hill

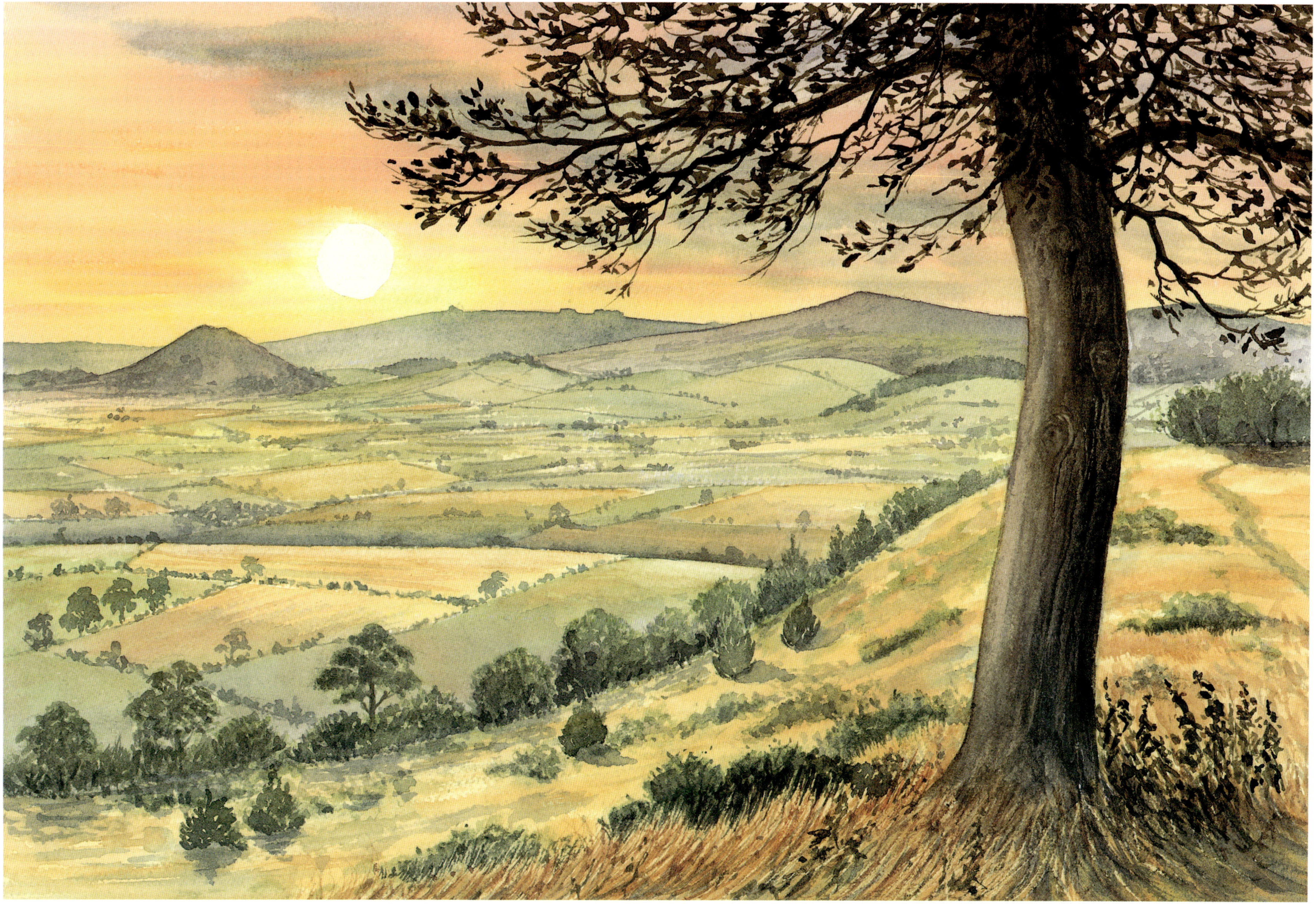

MY LOVE IS IN THE MOUNTIANS

My love is in the mountains dark and high
Where winds lie dead beneath an icy sky;
Where only the cold stars are intimate;
And tears are frozen in falling and voices die.

How shall I ever climb where my love is,
Out of life`s small and bright miscellanies,
To the unsullied mountains desolate -
From silences to deeper silences.

From the red tilth and the warm woods I go
Upward, and leave the meadows dear and low.
Seeing afar, when the cold hours grow late,
My love amid the hills of silver snow.

M. W.

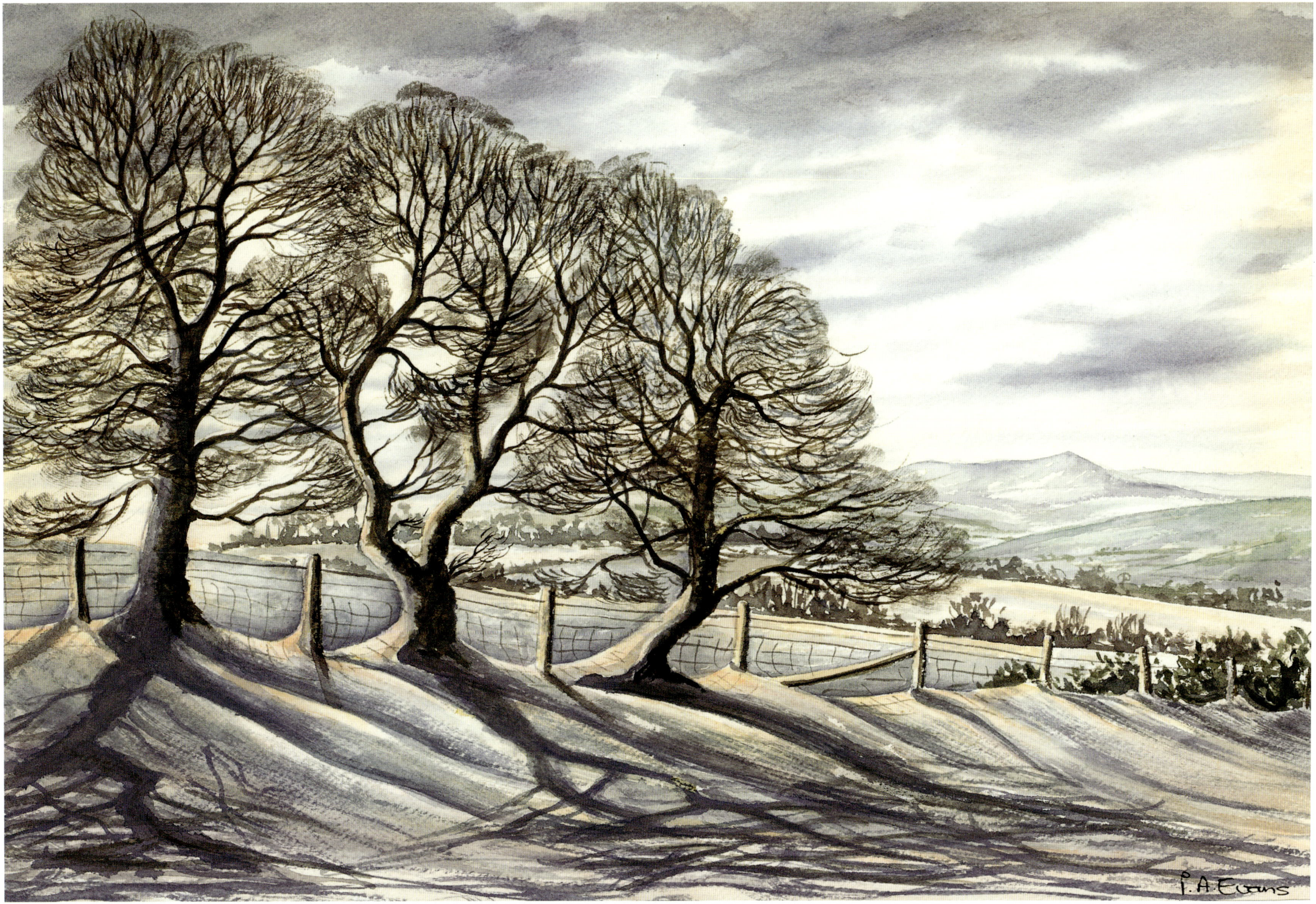

SNOWDROP TIME

Ah, hush! Tread softly through the rime,
For there will be a blackbird singing, or a thrush.
Like coloured beads the elm-buds flush:
All the trees dream of leaves and flowers and light,
And see! The northern bank is much more white
Than frosty grass, for now is snowdrop time

M. W.

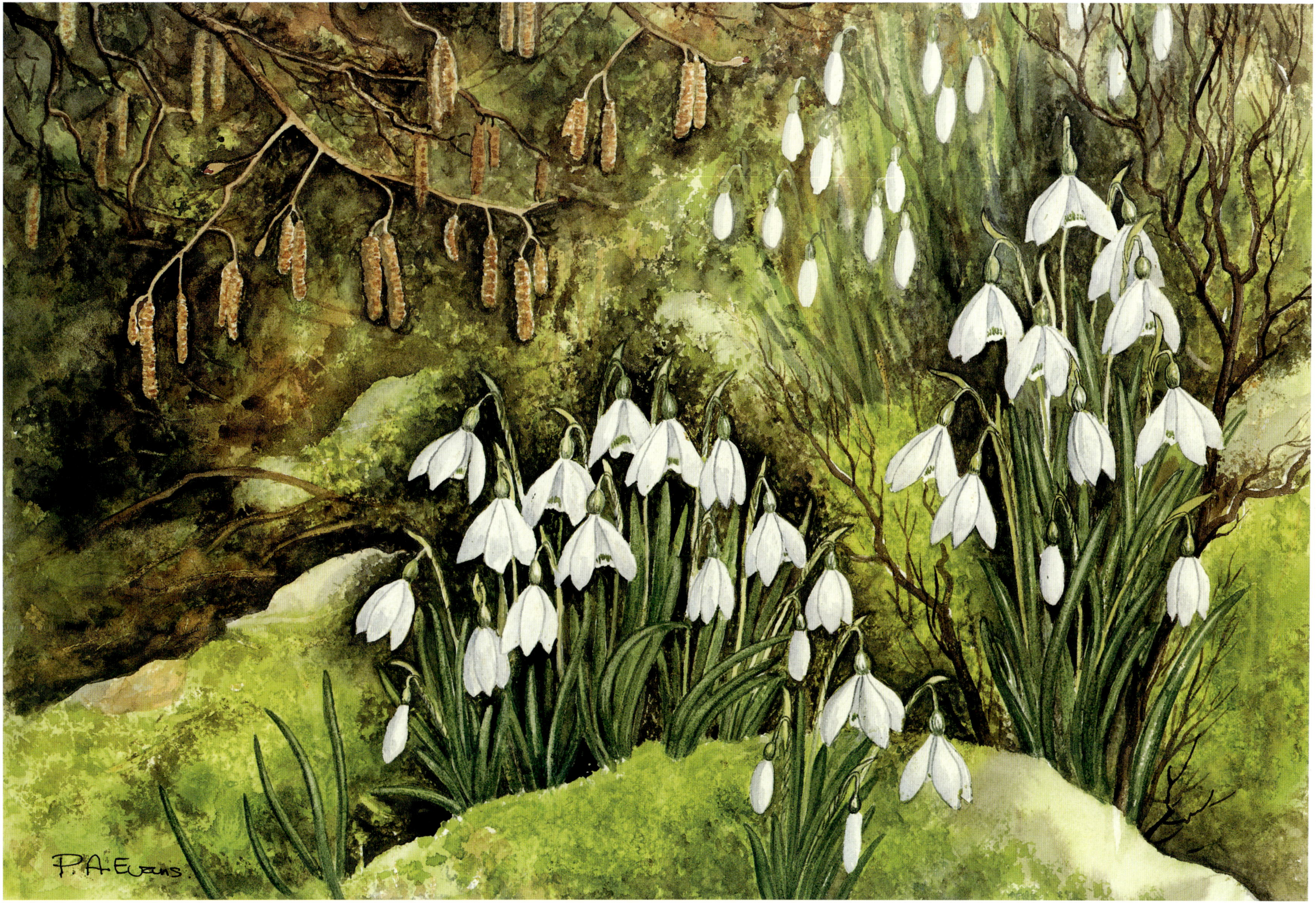
P. A. Evans

ROSE-BERRIES

The green pine-needles shiver glassily,
Each cased in ice. Harsh winter, grey and dun,
Shuts out the sun.
But with live, scarlet fire,
Enfolding seed of sweet Junes yet to be,
Rose-berries melt the snow, and burn above
The thorny briar,
Like beauty with its deathless seed of love.

M. W.

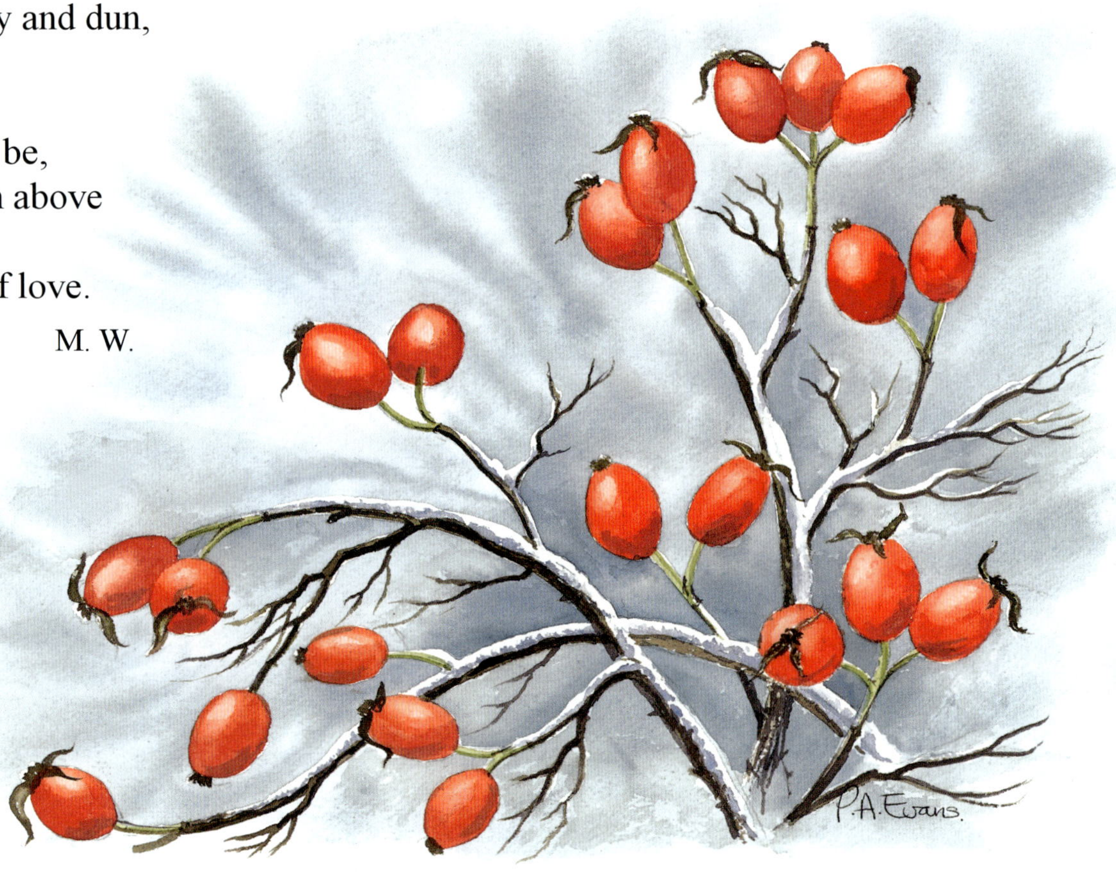

Rosehips

WINTER SUNRISE

All colors from the frozen earth have died,
And only shadow stains the cold, white snow:
But in the air the April tints abide;
Intangibly and radiantly they grow.
There bloom immortal crocuses, beside
A live-rose hedge, and irises that grow
Along a far green inlet – circling wide
Anemone fields where none but stars may go.
The ardours of a thousand springs are there;
Through infinite deeps they quicken, bright and tender:
In that sequestered garden of the air
No icy pall is heavy on the splendour.
Since you are not in the wintry world to love me,
How softly painted flushes Death above me!.

M. W.

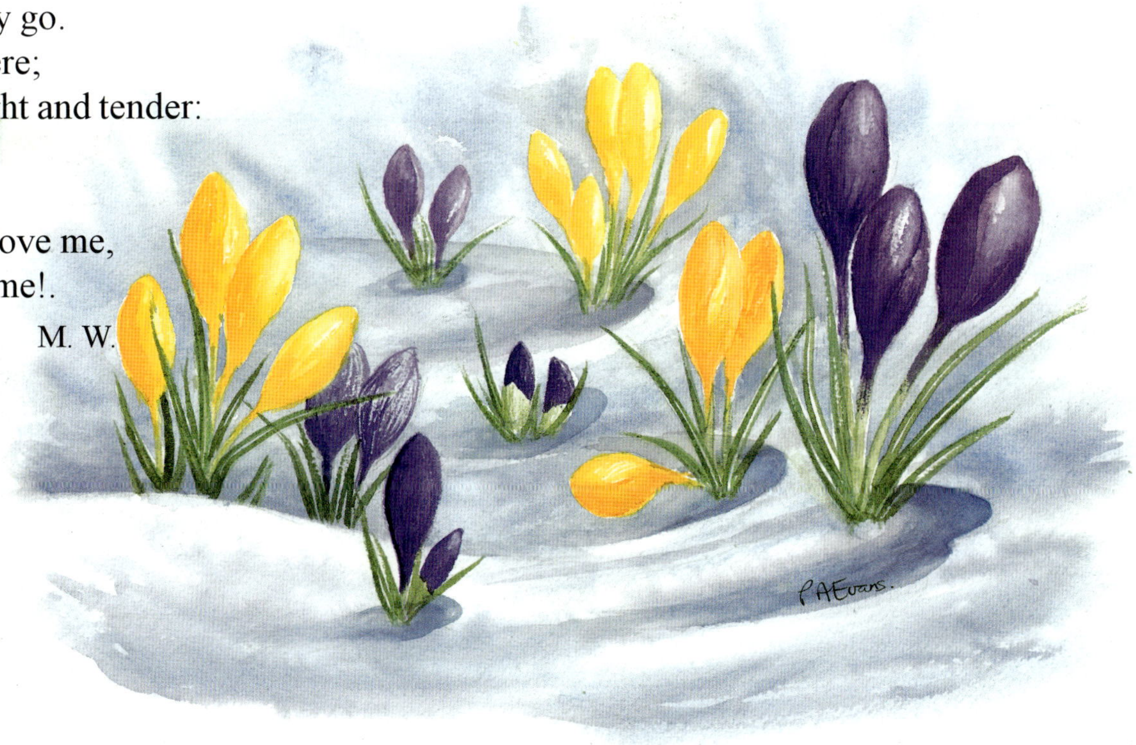

IN DARK WEATHER

Against the gaunt, brown-purple hill
The bright brown oak is wide and bare;
A pale-brown flock is feeding there -
Contented, still.

No bracken lights the bleak hill-side;
No leaves are on the branches wide;
No lambs across the fields have cried;
- Not yet.

But whorl by whorl the green fronds climb;
The ewes are patient till their time;
The warm buds swell beneath the rime -
For life does not forget.

M. W.

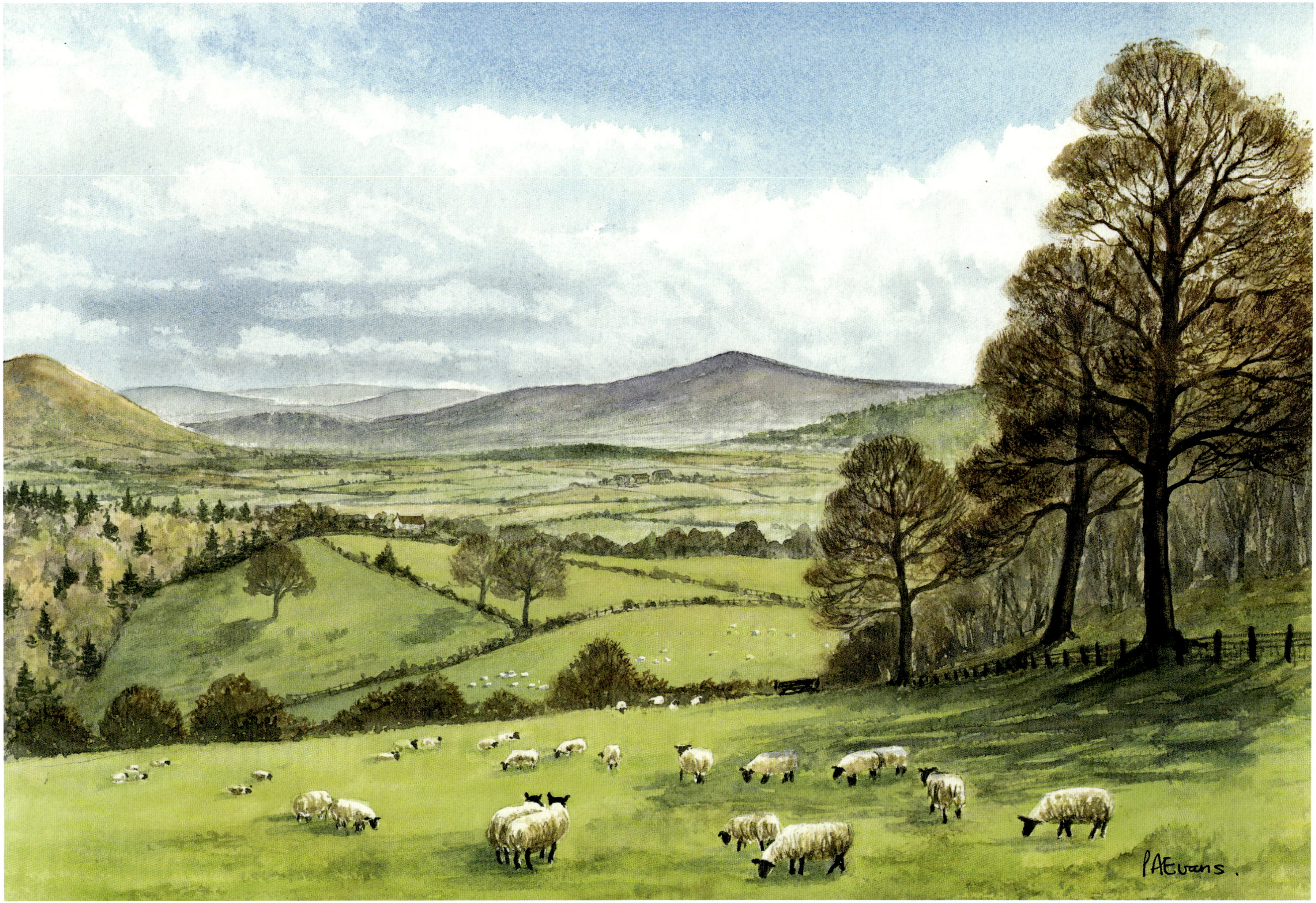
PAEvans.

THE PLAIN IN AUTUMN

A solemn land of long-fulfilled desires
Is this, and year by year the self-same fires
Burn in the trees. The untarnished colours keep
The sweetness of the young earth's infant sleep:
Beyond the plain, beneath the evening star,
The burnished hills like stately peacocks are.
Great storms march out. The flocks across the grass
Make their low plaint while the swift shadows pass:
Memoried deep in Hybla, the wild bee
Sings in the purple-fruited damson tree:
And, darkly sweet as Ruth, the dairy maid
By the lean, laughing shepherd is waylaid.

M. W.

Earls Hill, Pontesford Hill, Stiperstones and Bromlow Callow from Lea Cross

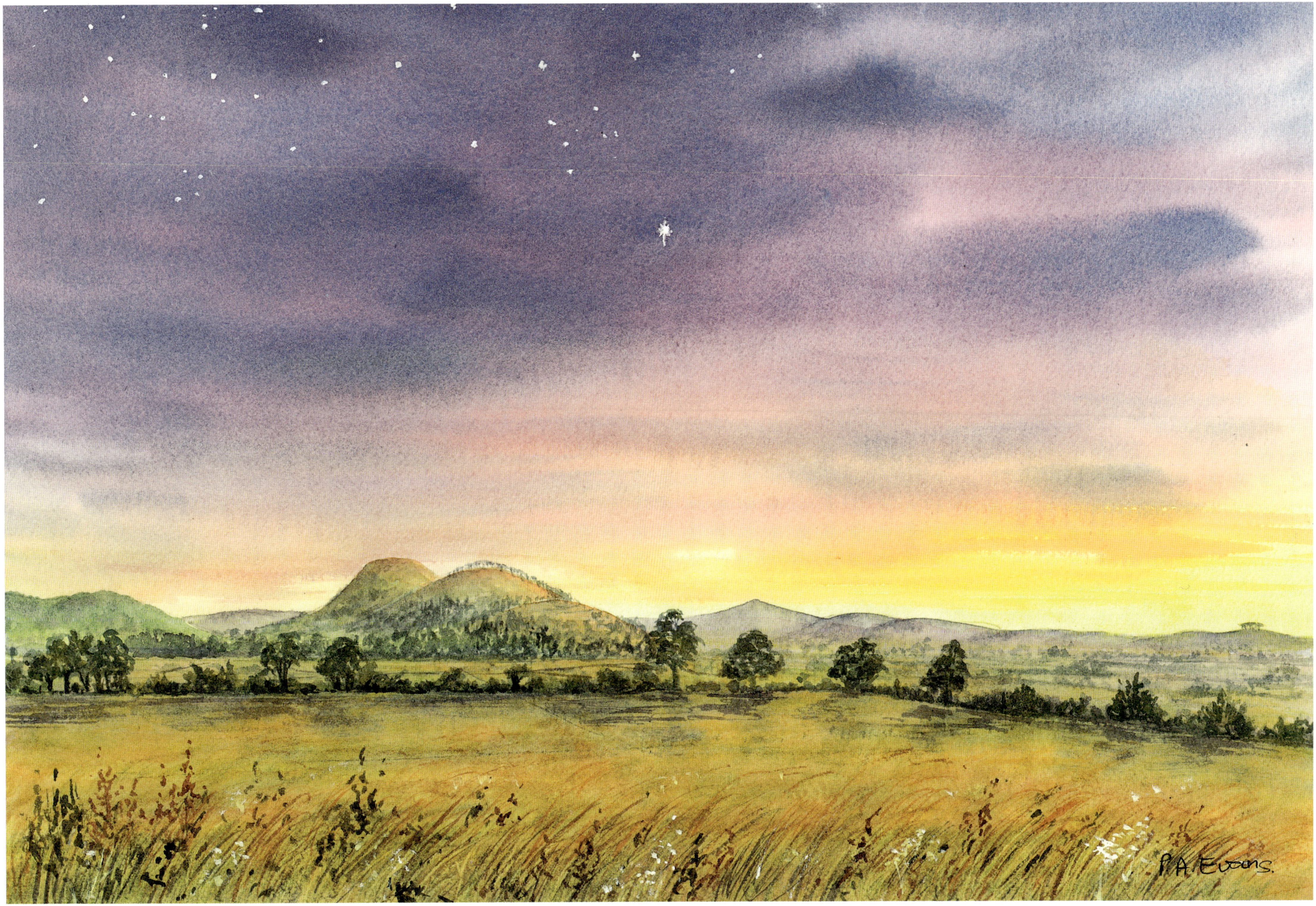
P.A. Evans.

ON RECEIVING A BOX OF SPRING FLOWERS IN LONDON

So the old, dear freemasonry goes on –
The busy life, the laughter-under-sod,
The leafy hosts with spear and gonfalon
Guarding the earthy mysteries of God.

I did not think the violets came so soon,
Yet here are five, and all my room is sweet;
And here's an aconite – a golden moon
Shining where all her raying leaflets meet;

And here a snowdrop, finely veined – ah, see!
Fresh from the artist's hand, and folded close:
She only waits the sunshine and the bee;
Then she will open like a golden rose.

M. W.

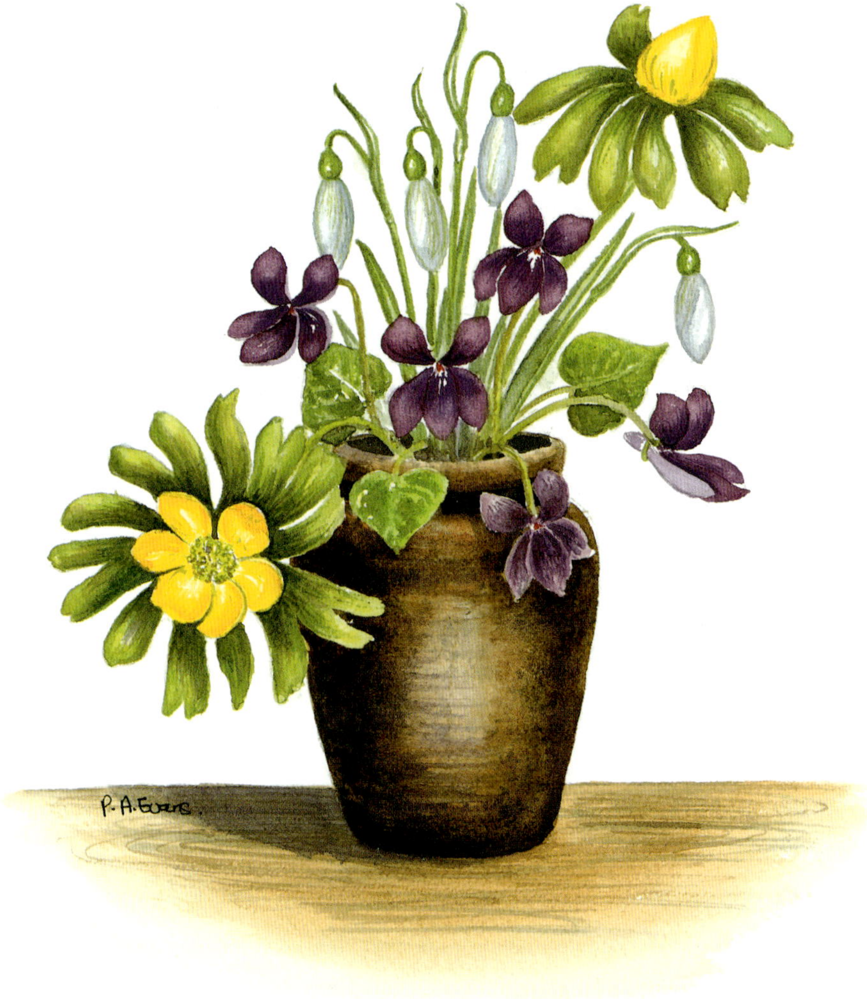

Opposite Ratlinghope Church (Slepe)

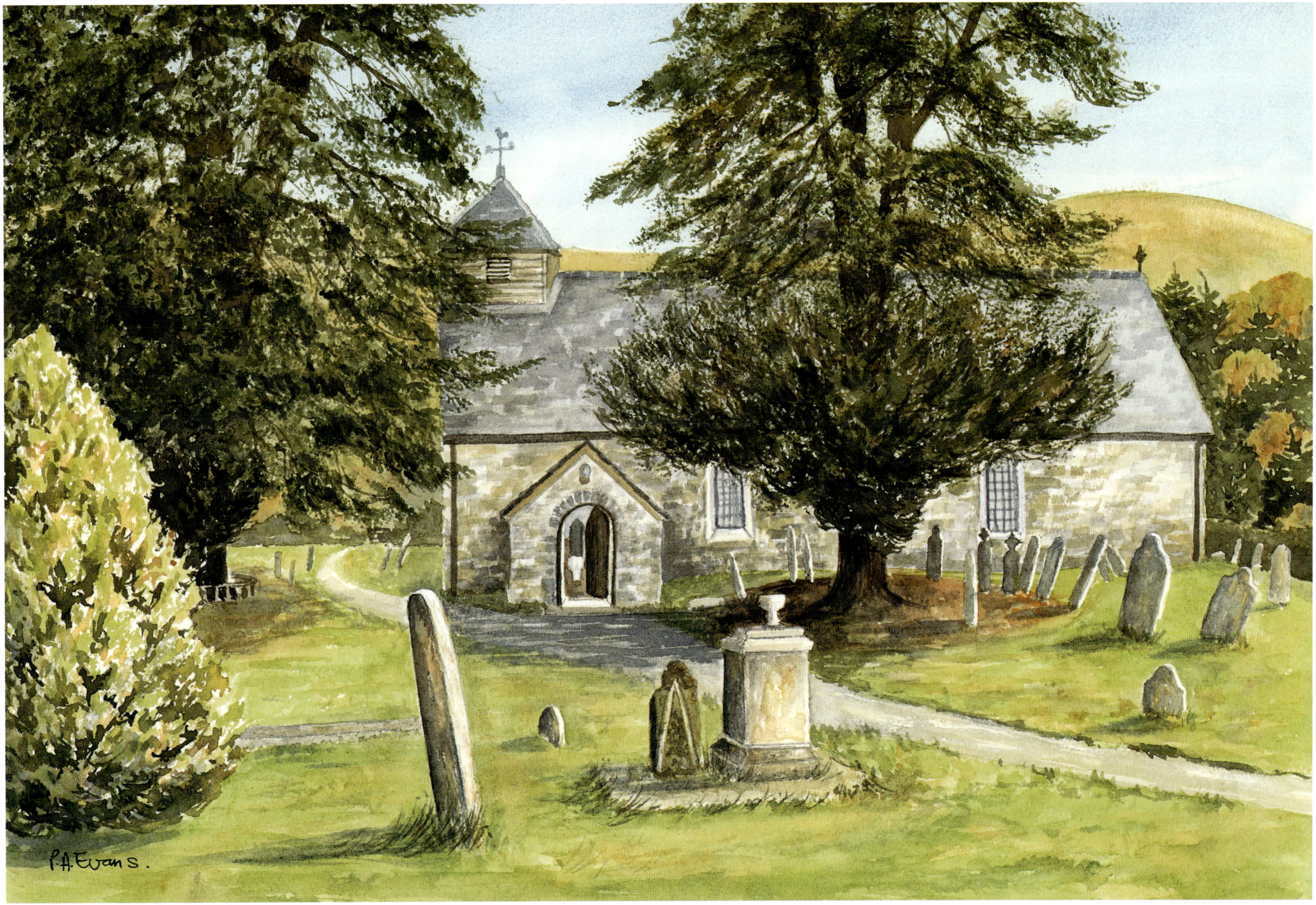
P.A.Evans.

SLEPE

Below, in a purple cup brimming with golden moonlight and covered by a lid of sky – jewelled like the cover of a wassail cup – lay the small, huddled village of Slepe. The church tower – grey, square, knowing all winds, all rains, all snows, and regarding them but as the beating of small birds against its massive walls – rose out of a tall rookery. A farm or two, the vicarage, the school where Deborah and Joe learnt their less useful knowledge, the post office and a few cottages – these were all the human outposts between the empty valley and the lonely hills.

from - *The Golden Arrow*

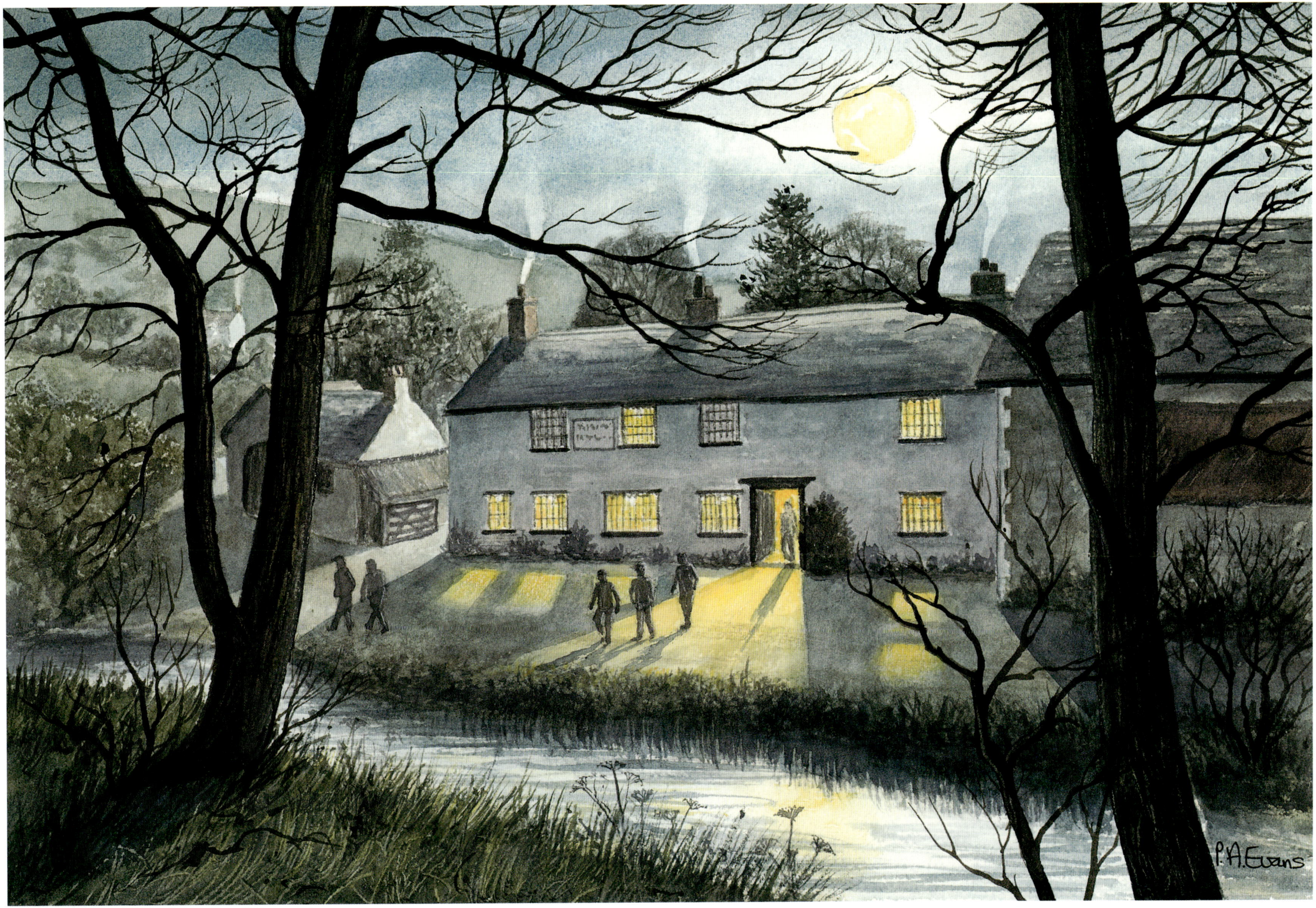
P.A.Evans

THRESHOLDS

So here is come the night of nights!
On every pine a star is kindled.
Too slowly cumbrous summer dwindled;
But now the frosty silence hums
And comfort in the boundless darkness comes
Along the heights.

Through weary times of brooding harm
We waited. Now the hour is ringing.
In haste we leave the wicket swinging
And whisper, splashing through the mire,
Of music and of colours bright like fire
At Thresholds Farm.

Up yonder on the hill-side stark
The long sheds crouch beneath the larches.
We smile to think the whole world marches
With us to where the shippen gleams
And flower-pale faces cluster, keen as dreams,
Against the dark.

We hear the cow-chains lift and fall;
We almost feel the ageless splendour
Of Child and Mother, warm and tender;
We run and softly push the door . . .
The mice go shrieking down the lonely floor,
The empty stall.

M. W.

Thresholds & Clee Hills from Cothercott Hill

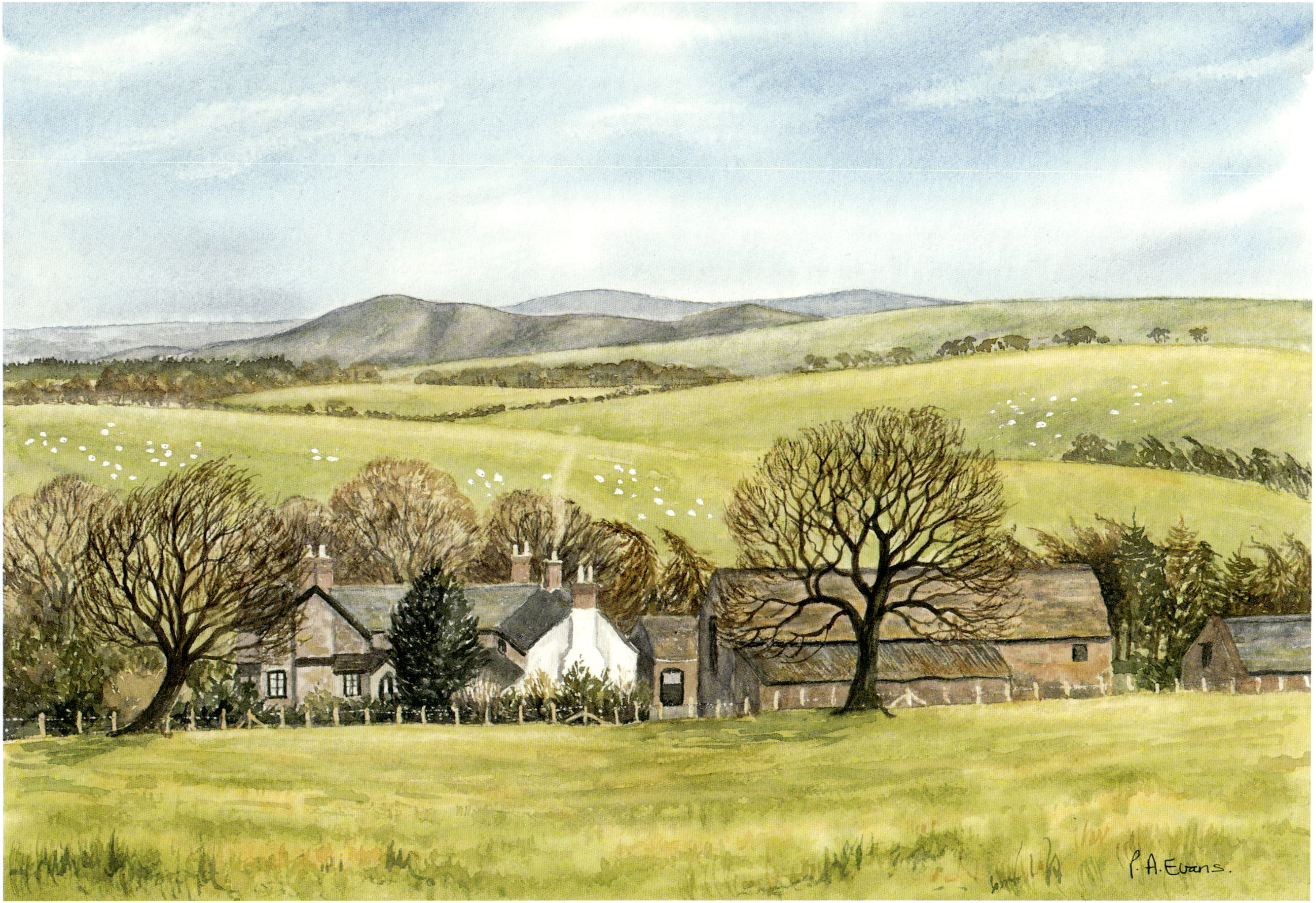
P. A. Evans.

CASTLE POLREBEC

On a summer afternoon, about milking time, you could not find a pleasanter place than this, our hall, with the door opened wide on the rolling woods, the sunlight streaming in, the air full of the fragrancy of aromatic leaves, blossoms and the flower of the grass, coming in heady and full of life…

It clung like a nest, this my garden, to the grey wall of our castle, and it was grey itself with the quiet greyness of doves…

from - *Armour Wherein He Trusted*

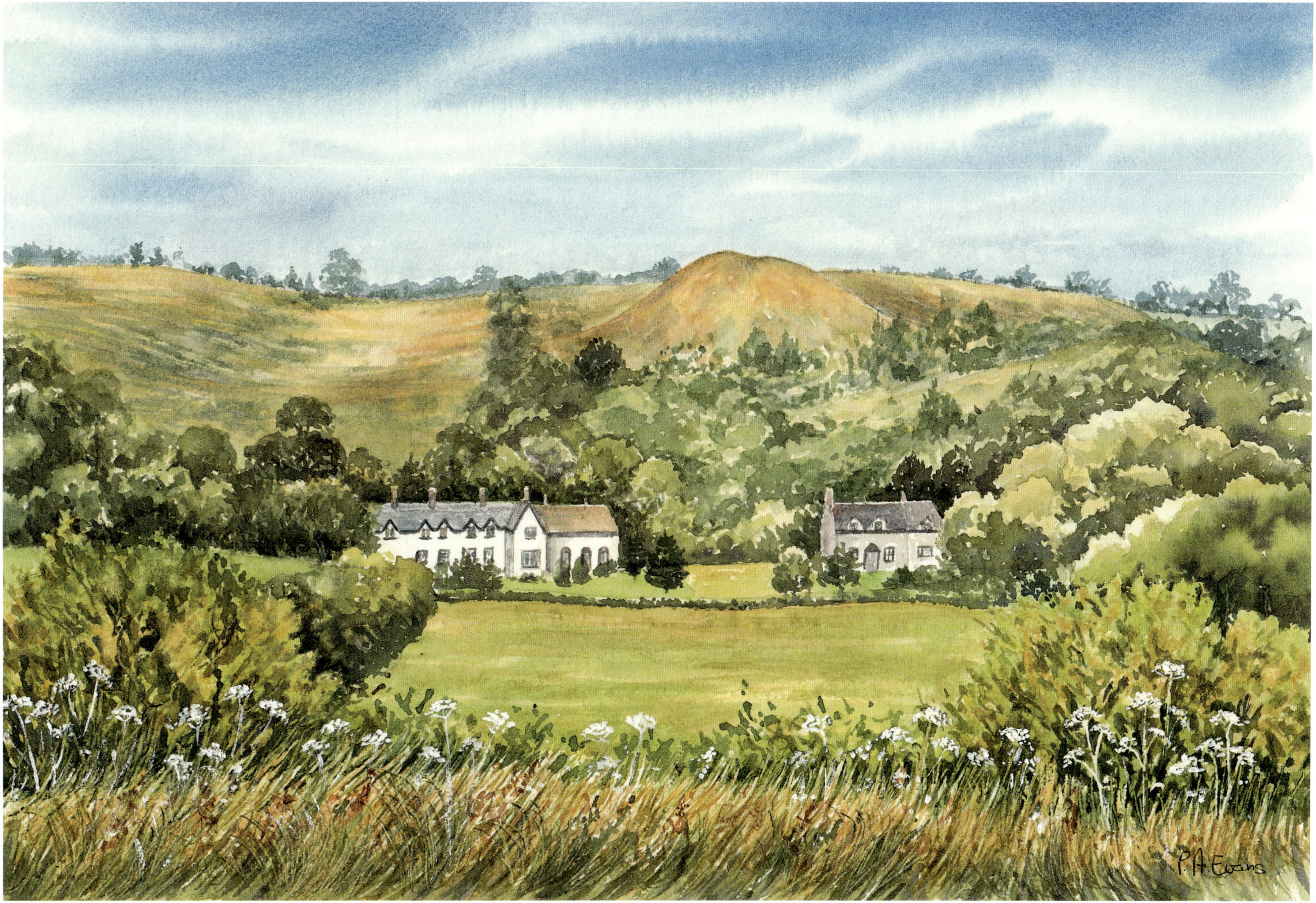
P.A. Evans

THE HAPPY LIFE

No silks have I, no furs nor feathers,
But one old gown that knows all weathers;
No veils nor parasols nor lace,
But rough hands and a tanned face.
Yet the soft crinkled leaves are mine
Where pale, mysterious veins shine,
And laced larches upon the blue,
And grey veils where the moon looks through;
The cries of birds across the lawns
In dark and teeming April dawns;
The sound of wings at the door-sill,
Where grows the wet-eyed tormentil;
The ripe berry's witcheries -
Its perfect round that satisfies;
And the gay scent of the wood I burn,
And the slap of butter in a busy churn.

M. W.

Barn Owl in Woodland near Stiperstones

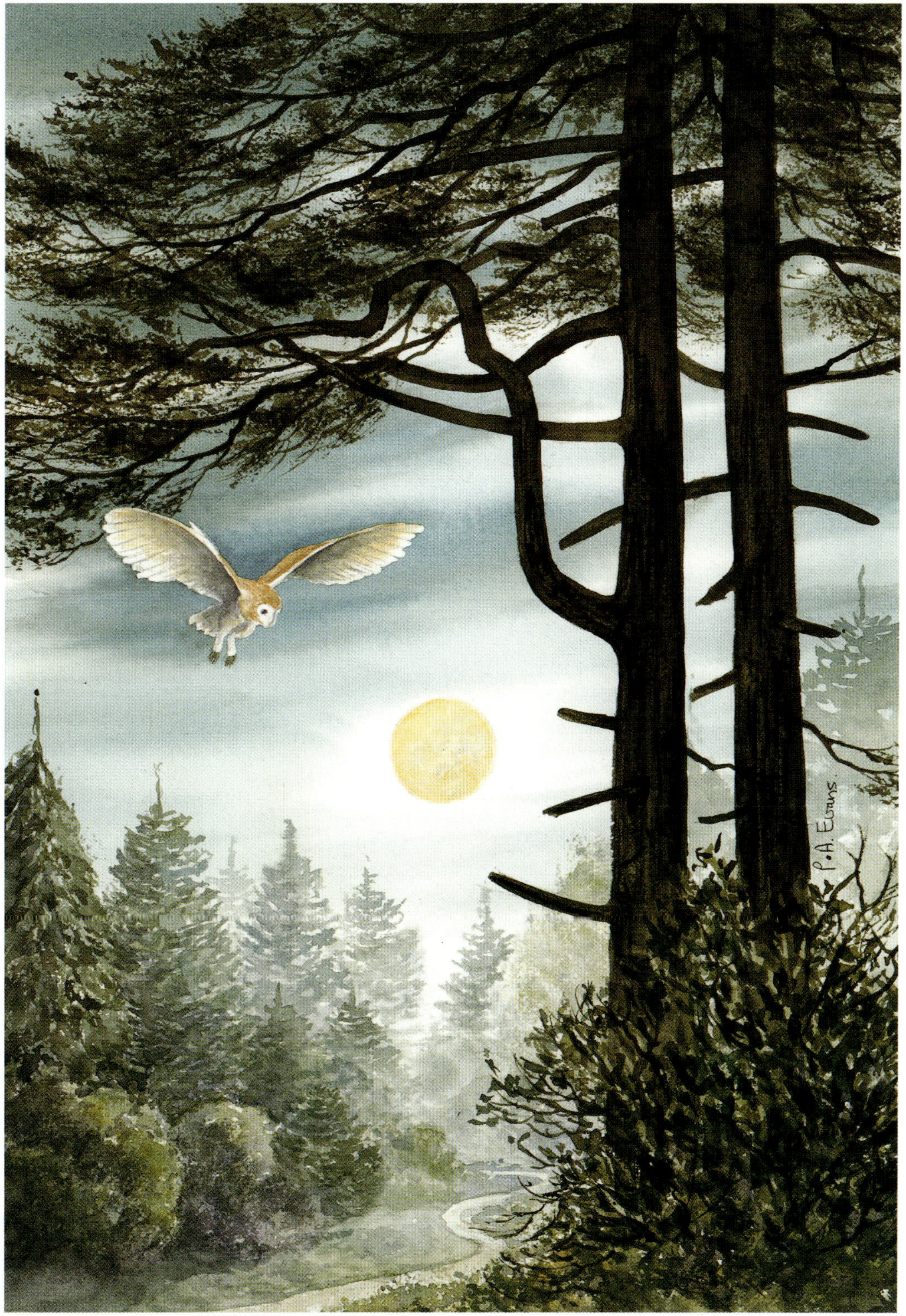
P.A. Evans

FOXGLOVES

The foxgloves bells, with lolling tongue,
Will not reveal what peals were rung
In Faery, in Faery,
A thousand ages gone.
All the golden clappers hang
As if but now the changes rang;
Only from the mottled throat
Never any echoes float.
Quite forgotten, in the wood,
Pale, crowded steeples rise;
All the time that they have stood
None has heard their melodies.
Deep, deep in wizardry
All the foxglove belfries stand.
Should they startle over the land,
None would know what bells they be.
Never any wind can ring them,
Nor the great black bees the swing them –
Every crimson bell, down-slanted,
Is so utterly enchanted.

M. W.

Foxgloves in Woodland near Stiperstones

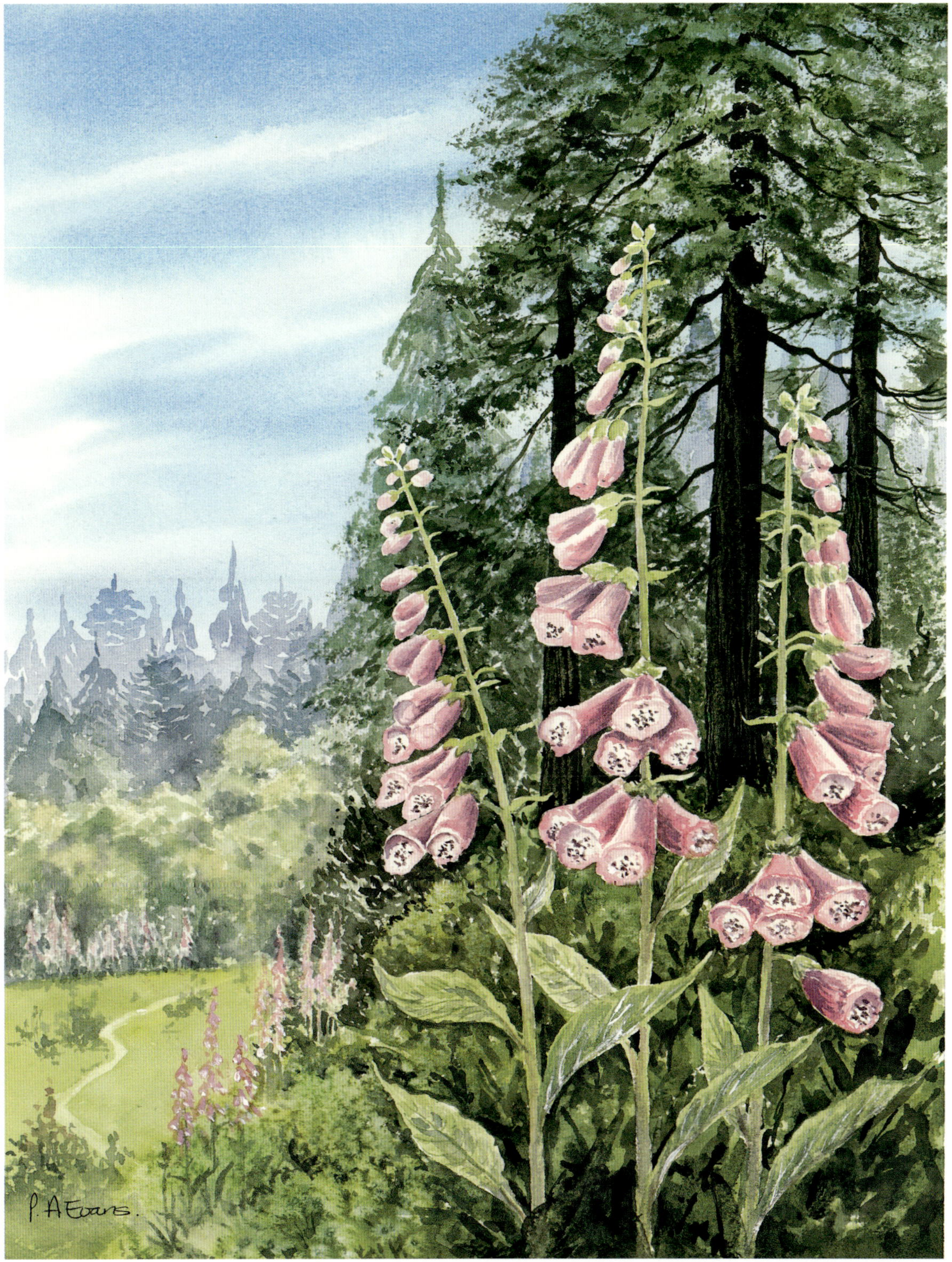
P. A Evans.

BOUNTY

The full woods overflow
Among the meadow's gold!
A blue-bell wave has rolled,
Where crowded cowslips grow.
The drifting hawthorn snow
Brims over hill and wold.
The full woods overflow
Among the meadow's gold;
The ditches are aglow!
The marshes cannot hold
Their kingcups manifold.
Heav'n's beauty crowds below,
The full woods overflow!

M. W.

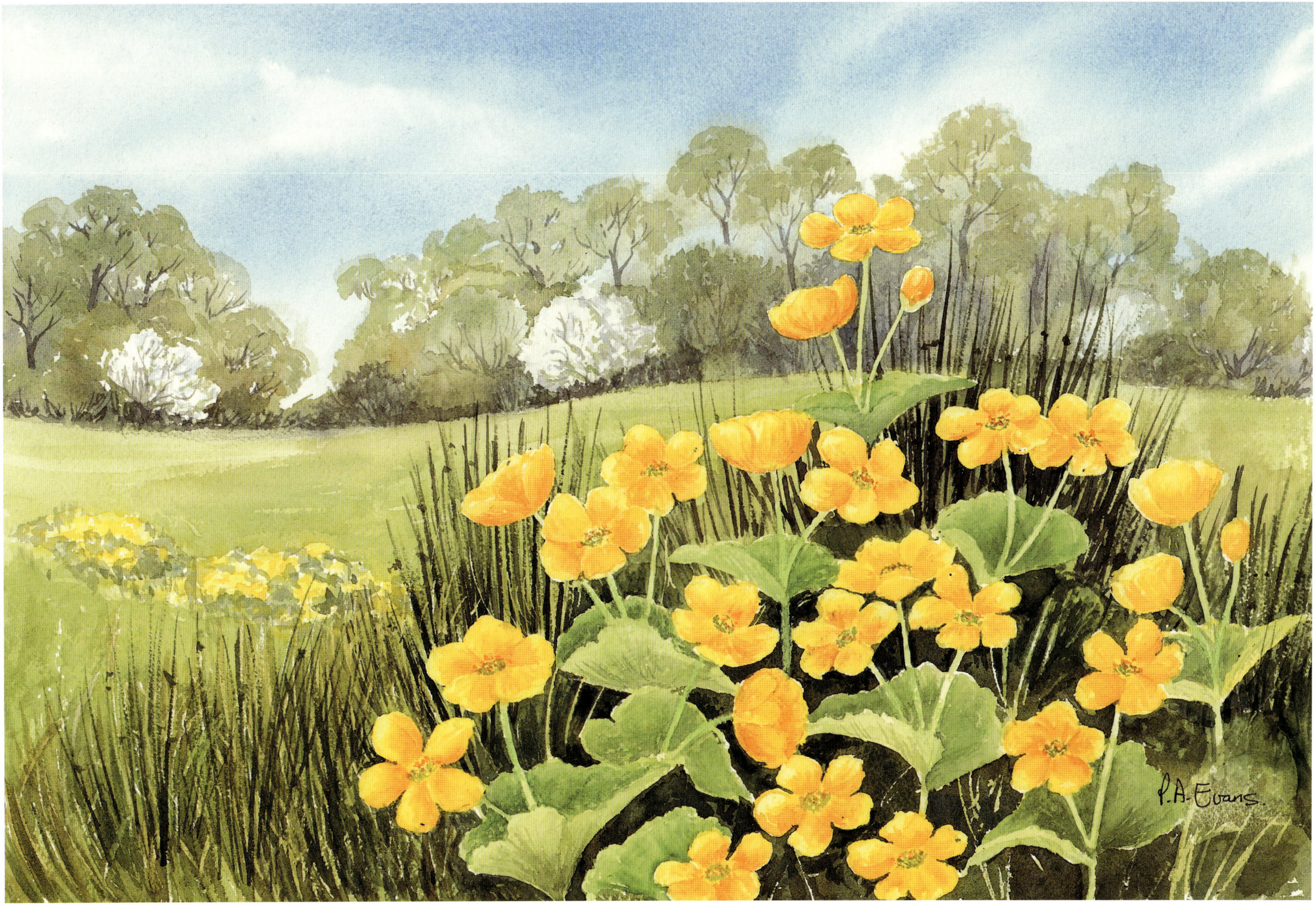
P.A. Evans.

HARVEST SONG

The noise of bells has sunk to rest;
The low grey clouds move swiftly on.
The land is still as Avalon,
Deep-breathing in its sleep, and blest.

For us the holy corn is spread
Across the quiet, misty dales
Towards the hyacinth hills of Wales,
To give our souls their daily bread.

For us that starling flock took wing,
And, like a silken banner blown,
Across the rippling corn has flown,
To teach our spirits how to sing.

A tiny hedge-bird chirps to me,
And down among the heart`s-ease pass
The lowly people of the grass;
They preach to me of charity.

M. W.

Middletown & Breidden Hills from Plealey

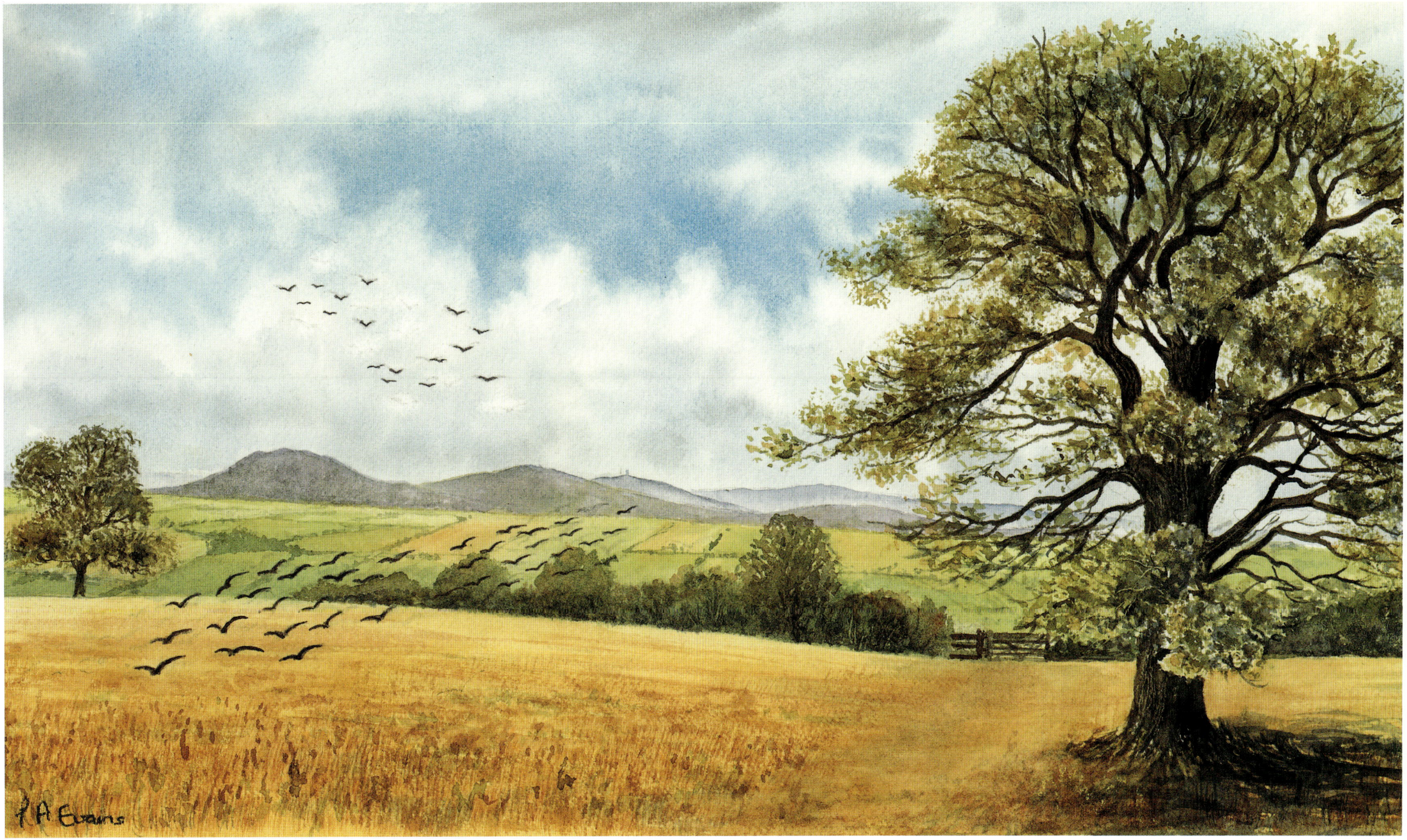

VIROCONIUM

Virocon – Virocon -
Still the ancient name rings on
And brings, in the untrampled wheat,
The tumult of a thousand feet.

Where trumpets rang and men marched by,
None passes but the dragon-fly.
Athwart the grassy town, forlorn,
The lone dor-beetle blows his horn.

The poppy standards droop and fall
Above one rent and mournful wall:
In every sunset-flame it burns,
Yet towers unscathed when day returns.

And still the breaking seas of grain
Flow havenless across the plain:
The years wash on, their spindrift leaps
Where the old city, dreaming, sleeps.

Grief lingers here, like mists that lie
Across the dawns of ripe July;
On capital and corridor
The pathos of the conqueror.

The pillars stand, with alien grace,
In churches of a younger race;
The chiselled column, black and rough,
Becomes a roadside cattle-trough:

The skulls of men who, right or wrong,
Still wore the splendour of the strong,
Are shepherds‘ lanterns now, and shield
Their candles in the lambing field.

But when, through evening‘s open door,
Two lovers tread the broken floor,
And the wild-apple petals fall
Round passion‘s scarlet festival;

When cuckoos call from the green gloom
Where dark, shelving forests loom;
When foxes bark beside the gate,
And the grey badger seeks his mate -

There haunts within them secretly
One that lives while empires die,
A shrineless god whose songs abide
Forever in the countryside.

M.W.

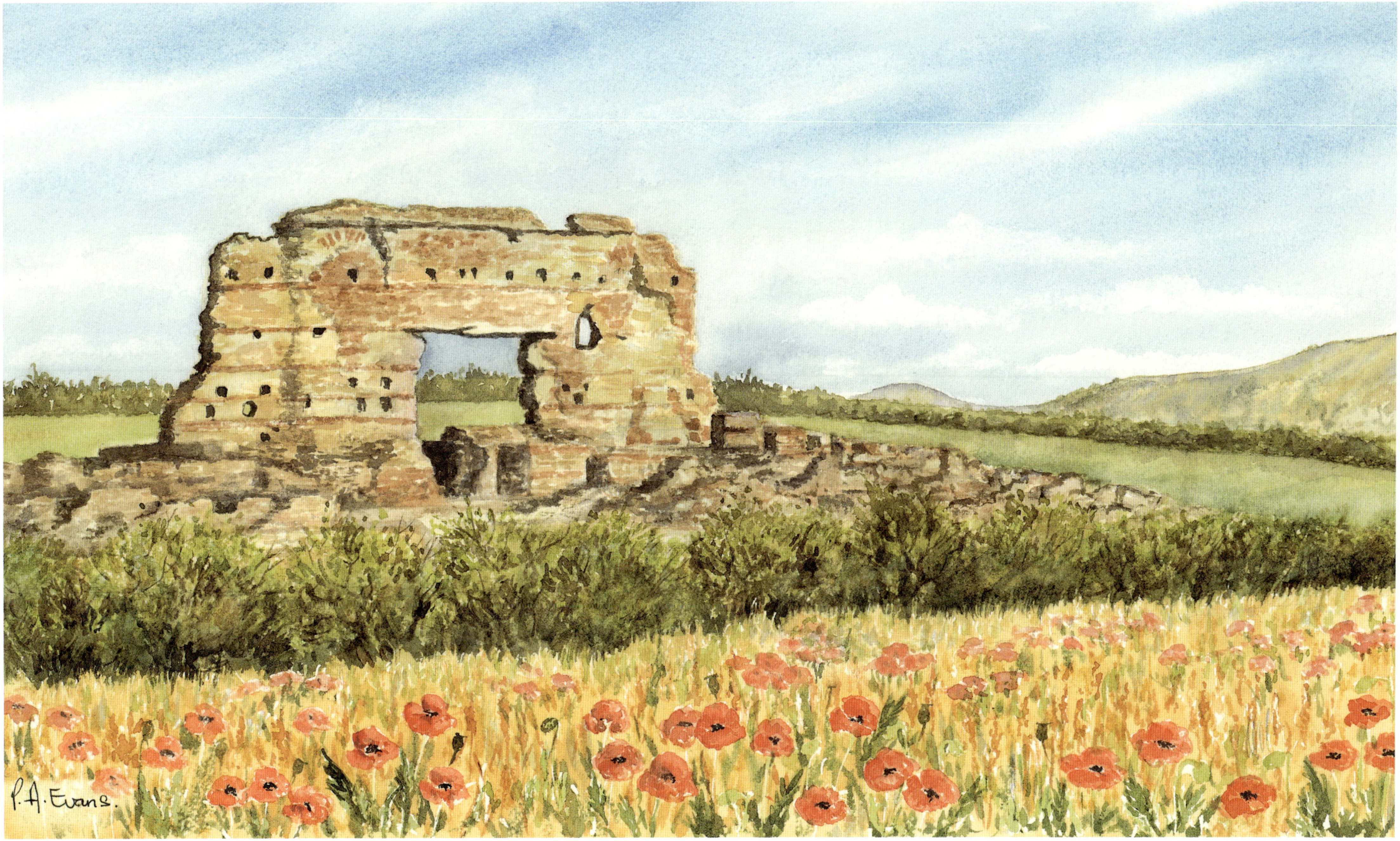
P.A. Evans.

SUNSET

Dull is the sun as an old lanthorn guttering,
And wild the valleys where the coughing sheep,
With wool torn by the brambles, climb and leap.
Here on the hill-top the old wind is uttering
His ancient, weary, unassuaged complaints,
Baying among the rocks that rise like tombs;
Shouting aloud the wild and secret dooms
Of all things living, while the evening faints
Amid the torn white flocks of cloud that fly
In panic all across the western sky.

M.W.

View from Manstone, Stiperstones towards Bromlow Callow & Wales

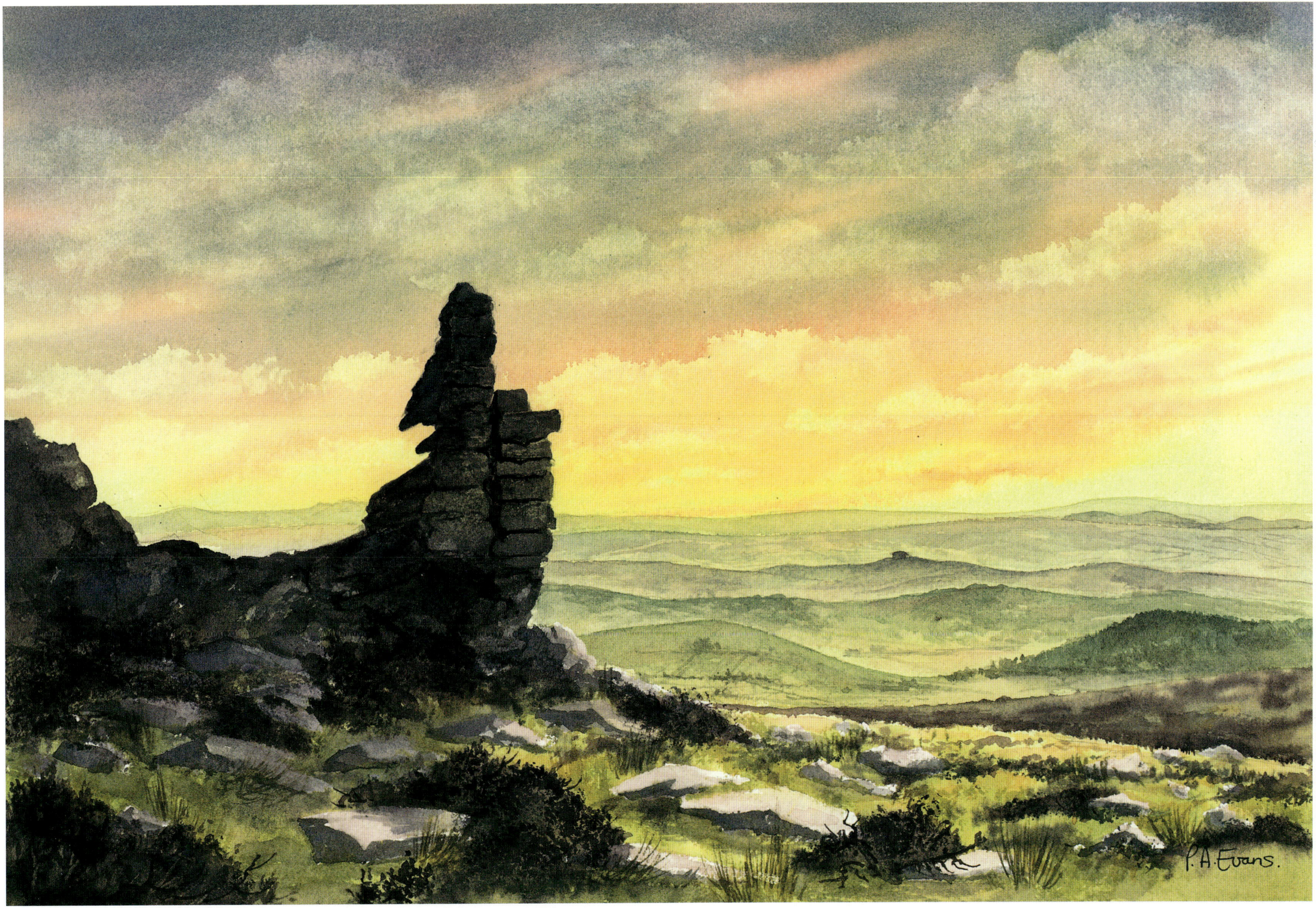
P. A. Evans.

THE DEVIL`S CHAIR – STIPERSTONES

For miles around, in the plains, the valleys, the mountain dwellings it was feared. It drew the thunder, people said. Storms broke round it suddenly out of a clear sky; it seemed almost as if it created storm. No one cared to cross the range near it after dark - when the black grouse laughed sardonically and the cry of a passing curlew shivered like broken glass. The sheep that inhabited these hills would, so the shepherds said, cluster suddenly and stampede for no reason, if they had grazed too near it in the night. So the throne stood - black massive, untenanted, yet with a well-worn air. It had the look of a chair from which the occupant has just risen, to which he will shortly return. It was understood that only when vacant could the throne be seen.

from *The Golden Arrow*

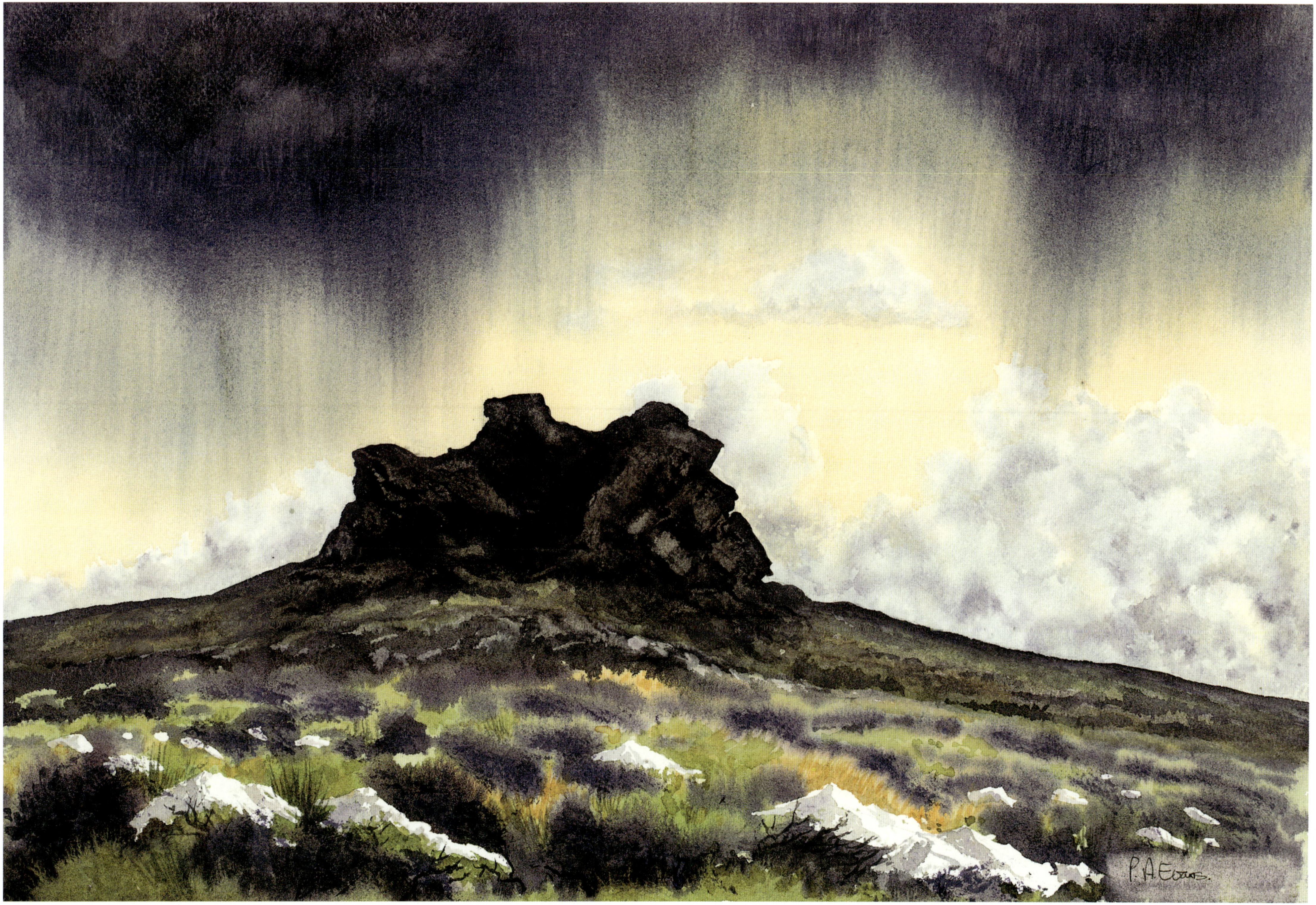
P.A.Evans.

THE NIGHT SKY (1916)

The moon, beyond her violet bars,
From towering heights of thunder-cloud,
Sheds calm upon our scarlet wars,
To soothe a world so small, so loud.
And little clouds like feathered spray,
Like rounded waves on summer seas,
Or frosted panes on a winter day,
Float in the dark blue silences.
Within their foam, transparent, white,
Like flashing fish the stars go by
Without a sound across the night.
In quietude and secrecy
The white, soft lightnings feel their way
To the boundless dark and back again,
With less stir than a gnat makes
In its joy, its little pain.

M. W.

Stiperstones Ridge looking over South Shropshire

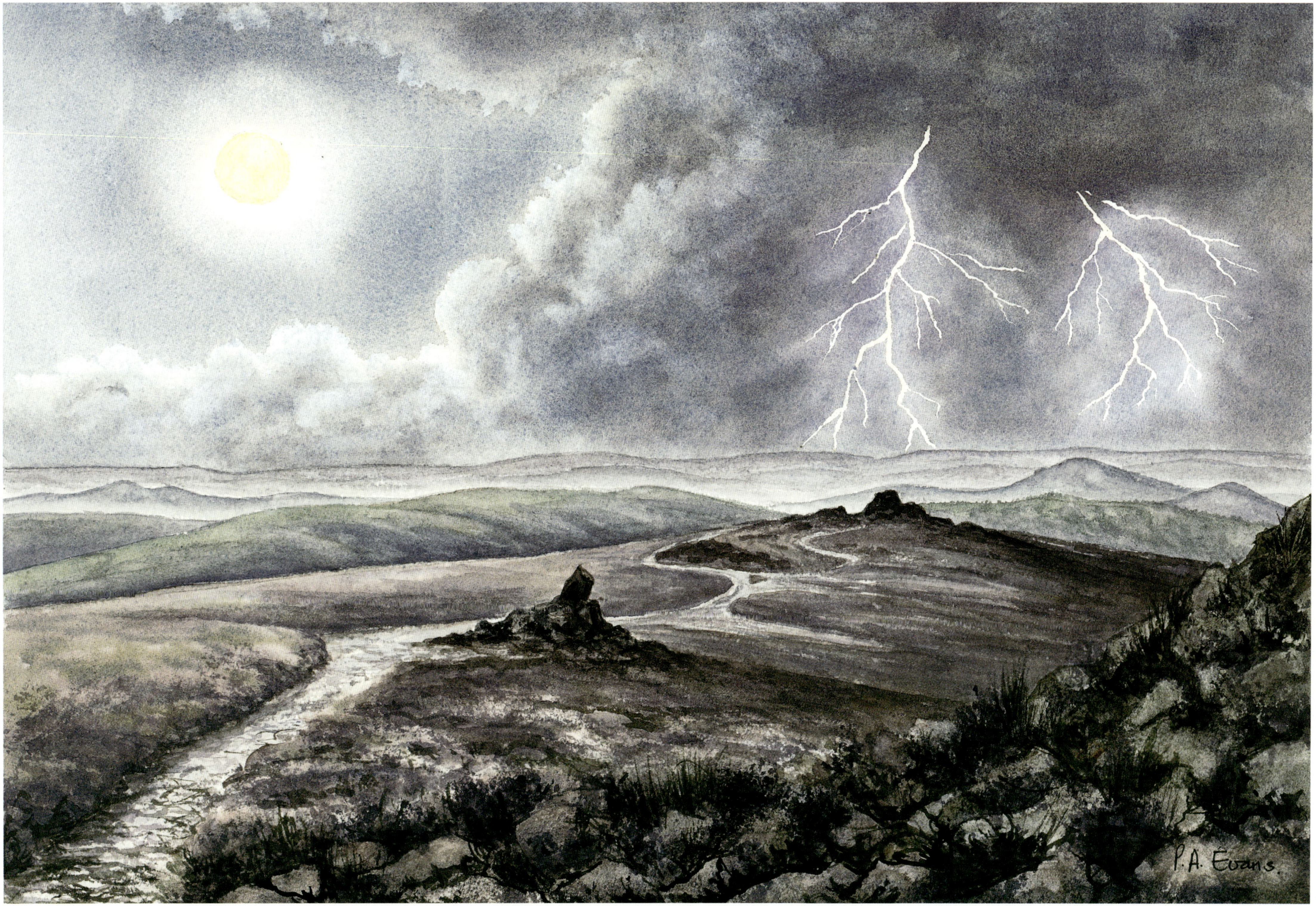
P.A. Evans

ON THE HILLS

Buffet on sweet buffet, the wildwood came,
Like a green wave or a green flame,
With melodies
And delicate fragrances
And the secret souls of the watching trees.

Colour on grave colour sleeps the ancient moor,
With its blue roof and its purple floor -
Where small birds fly
With merry, pencilled eye,
And like great gods the stately clouds go by.

M.W.

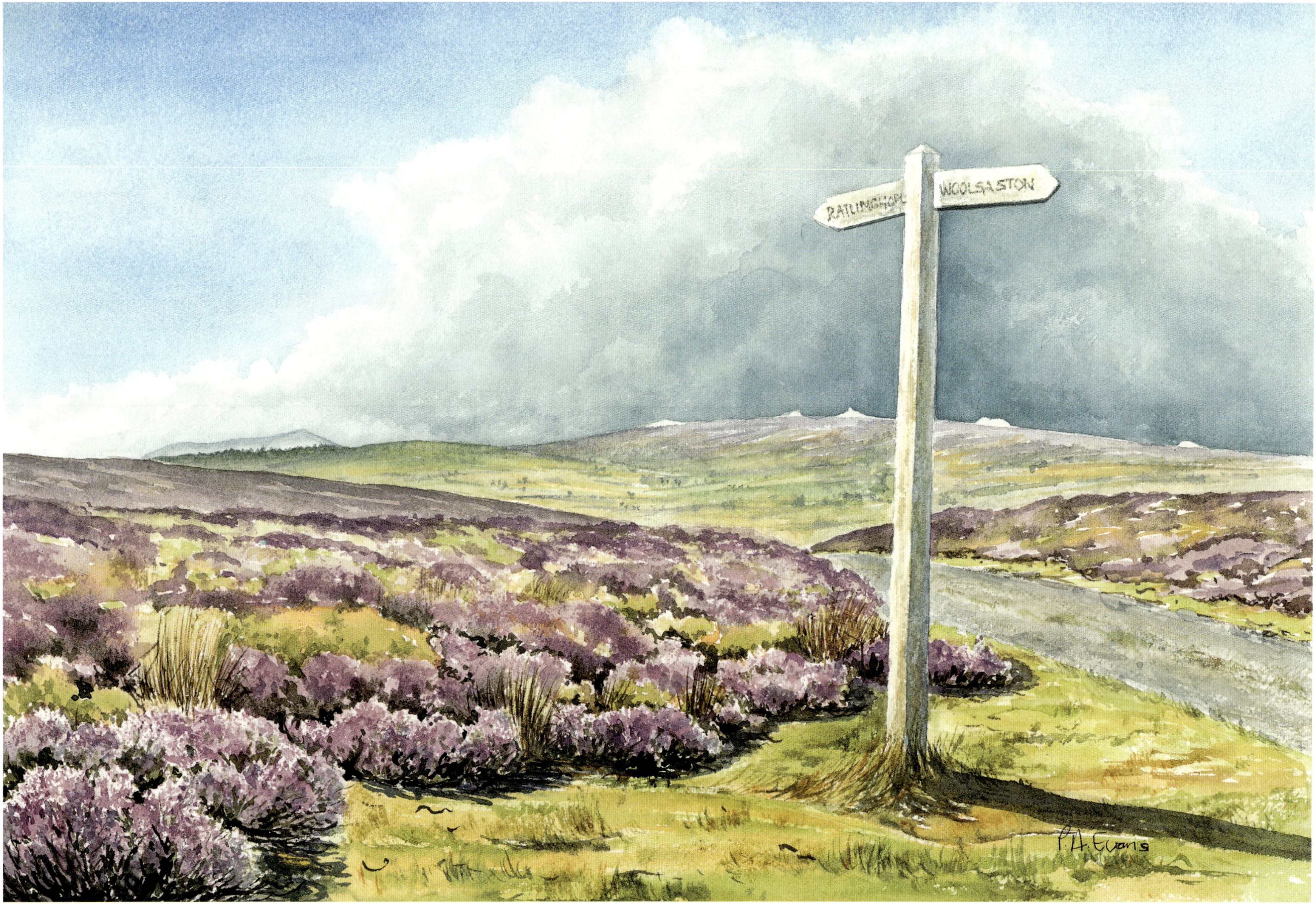
WOOLSASTON
P.A. Evans

THE SPIRIT OF EARTH

Love me – and I will give into your hands
The rare, enamelled jewels of my lands,
Flowers red and blue,
Tender with air and dew.

From far green armouries of pools and meres
I'll reach for you my lucent sheaves of spears -
The singing falls,
Where the lone ousel calls.

When, like a passing light upon the sea,
Your wood-bird soul shall clap her wings and flee,
She shall but nest
More closely in my breast.

M.W.

Cole Mere, North Shropshire

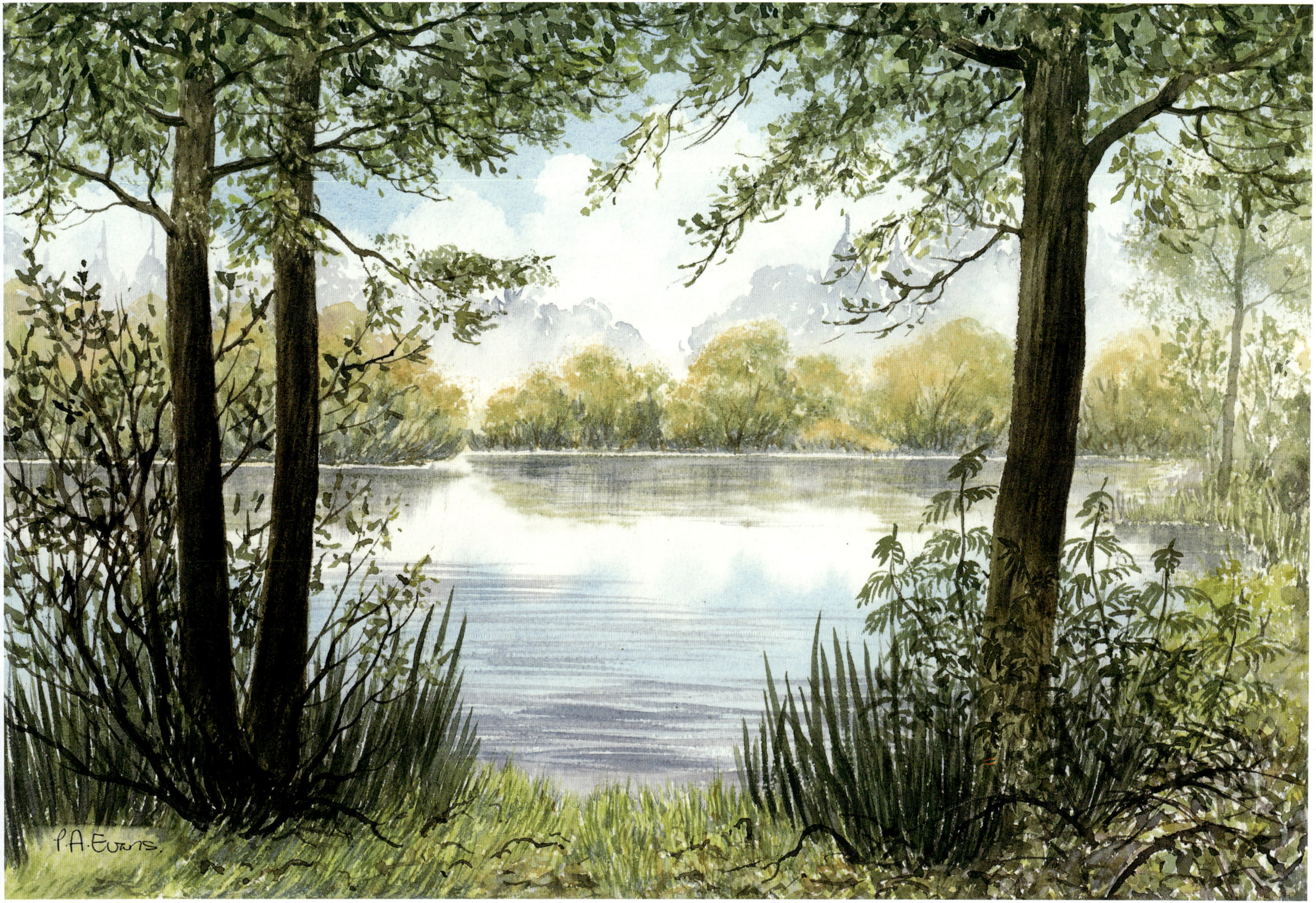
P.A. Evans.